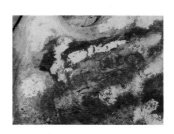

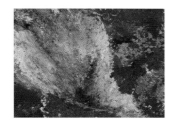

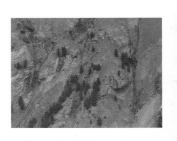

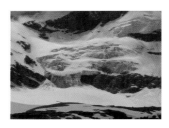

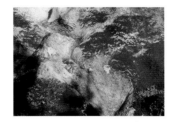

Yutaka Sone

The Renaissance Society at The University of Chicago
Aspen Art Museum
Kunsthalle Bern

Contents/Inhalt

Foreword

This book is a companion publication to three seminal exhibitions of Japanese artist Yutaka Sone (1965, Shizuoka, Japan; living in the US) held in the time-span of half a year, at The Renaissance Society at The University of Chicago, Illinois, the Aspen Art Museum, Colorado and the Kunsthalle Bern, Switzerland.

Sone's marked predilection for the impossible and the paradoxical is expressed in very diverse work that has its roots in performance but emphasizes the sculptural. Landscape and amusement inform an experience-oriented body of work that is cause for reconsidering our relationship with nature.

Forecast: Snow, the multimedia installation Sone conceived for The Renaissance Society presented the definitive collection of a group of works the artist has been developing in recent years in which he envisions snowflake patterns as blueprints for architectural spaces and psychological states, transforming their crystallized forms into fields and structures. Encompassing drawings, sculptural studies, natural crystal and white marble snowflake sculptures and paintings, the show was set in a wintery forest in the gallery with 100 pine trees and artificial snow. *X-Art Show* at the Aspen Art Museum concentrated on Sone's works fusing art with sport, performance and entertainment and featured snow-inspired paintings and sculptures, along with performance related ephemera, objects, film and photographs. A highlight of the exhibition was the collaboration between the Aspen Skiing Company and the museum. Sone's painting *Ski Madonna* was featured on all lift tickets for the 2005-2006 ski season and a pair of artist-designed eight-foot-cubed dice was transported from the museum to Buttermilk Mountain and tossed down the giant half pipe. Afterwards they were returned to the museum to become part of the exhibition. With *Like Looking for Snow Leopard* at the Kunsthalle Bern, Sone continues a physical and metaphorical journey towards an "unreachable place", creating works based on a personal assessment of landscape. He shows a new version of his very large multimedia landscape-piece entitled *It Seems Snow Leopard Island*. The installation comes along with a series of works made over the last several years: snowflake sculptures, topographic marble renderings of Los Angeles highway junctions, paintings, drawings and videowork. The show at the Kunsthalle Bern is the most extensive presentation of Sone's work in Europe thus far.

This ambitious series of exhibitions and publication would not have been possible without the much-valued support of many dedicated people.

At The Renaissance Society, *Forecast: Snow* was made possible with funding from the Zell Family Foundation. Additional exhibition sponsors include the Sara Lee Foundation and the Japan Foundation. This catalogue was generously funded by Bert A. Lies, Jr. and Rosina Lee Yue, with additional support from the W.L.S. Spencer Foundation.

X-Art Show was organized by the Aspen Art Museum and was underwritten by Amy and John Phelan with additional funding from the AAM National Council. The catalogue was underwritten by Bert A. Lies, Jr. and Rosina Lee Yue and Vicki and Kent Logan. Additional support was provided by Aspen Magazine.

The Kunsthalle Bern wishes to thank the Japan Foundation and the Stanley Thomas Johnson Foundation for making this exhibition and catalogue possible through their support. We would also like to thank the City and Canton of Bern, the SRG SSR Idée Suisse and the Club 15 for their continuous commitment to the Kunsthalle program.

This book attempts to draw out some of the background to Yutaka Sone's remarkable work, and for this we are indebted to Benjamin Weissman, who enjoys ongoing ski adventures with Yutaka Sone and who has written a delightful text enriching our understanding of the artist's deliberate mix of fiction and reality. Hamza Walker, Director of Education and Associate Curator at The Renaissance Society, focused his essay on Sone's recent series of marble snowflake sculptures, contextualizing them within the history of both art and science via their relationship to the project of Wilson A. Bentley, whose photographic collection of individual snowflakes typifies an era when cultural and scientific representation had more in common.

We are also grateful to Nina Oeghoede for her considerate editorial coordination and Kim Beirnaert for her sensitive approach to the design of this publication. A special word of thanks goes to Min Nishihara, and the artist's assistants Sky Burchard, Michael Bauer, Larissa Brantner James and Lauren Mollica. Thanks are also due to the artist's gallerist David Zwirner and his collaborator Hanna Schouwink for their generous commitment to this project. Our final thank you goes to Yutaka Sone, a remarkable artist whose energetic enthusiasm has made this project a superb journey for all of us.

> Susanne Ghez, Director and Chief Curator,
> The Renaissance Society at The University of Chicago
>
> Heidi Zuckerman Jacobson, Director and Chief Curator,
> Aspen Art Museum
>
> Philippe Pirotte, Director and Chief Curator,
> Kunsthalle Bern

Vorwort

Diese Publikation versteht sich als Reisebegleiter für drei Einzelausstellungen des japanischen Künstlers Yutaka Sone (1965 in Shizuoka geboren, lebt in den USA), die während der Zeitspanne eines halben Jahres gezeigt wurden in The Renaissance Society at The University of Chicago, Illinois, dem Aspen Art Museum, Colorado und der Kunsthalle Bern, Schweiz.

Sones ausgeprägte Vorliebe für das Unmögliche und das Paradoxe findet ihren Ausdruck in einem sehr breit gefächerten Werk, das seine Wurzeln in der Performance hat, den Schwerpunkt jedoch auf die Plastik setzt. Landschaft und Vergnügen formen ein am Erleben orientiertes Werk, das uns veranlasst, unser Verhältnis zur Natur neu zu überdenken.

Forecast: Snow, die Multimedia-Installation, die Sone für The Renaissance Society entworfen hat, präsentierte die definitive Versammlung einer in den vergangenen Jahren entwickelten Werkgruppe, worin der Künstler Schneeflockenstrukturen als Schnittmuster für architektonischen Raum und psychische Zustände behandelt, indem er ihre kristallinen Formen in Felder und Bauten verwandelt. Die Ausstellung umfasste Zeichnungen, plastische Studien, Naturkristall- und weiße Marmorskulpturen von Schneeflocken sowie Gemälde und war in einen winterlichen Wald aus 100 Kiefern und künstlichem Schnee installiert. *X-Art Show* am Aspen Art Museum konzentrierte sich auf Arbeiten Sones, die Kunst mit Sport, Performance und Entertainment vereinen, und zeigte von Schnee inspirierte Gemälde und Skulpturen sowie auf Performance bezogene Ephemera, Objekte, Filme und Fotografien. Ein Höhepunkt der Ausstellung bildete die Kooperation zwischen der Aspen Skiing Company und dem Museum. Sones Gemälde *Ski Madonna* zierte sämtliche Lift-Tickets der Skisaison 2005-2006 und ein Paar vom Künstler entworfene, über zwei Meter große Würfel wurden vom Museum nach Buttermilk Mountain transportiert und dort die gigantische Half-Pipe hinuntergeworfen. Anschließend brachte man sie ins Museum zurück, wo sie Teil der Ausstellung wurden. Mit *Like Looking for Snow Leopard* in der Kunsthalle Bern führt Sone eine physische und metaphorische Reise zu einem "unerreichbaren Ort" fort, indem er Arbeiten geschaffen hat, die auf einer persönlichen Einschätzung von Landschaft fußen. Er zeigt eine neue Version seines sehr großen Multimedia Landschaftsstücks *It Seems Snow Leopard Island*. Die Installation erscheint zusammen mit einer Reihe von Arbeiten, die während der letzten Jahre entstanden sind: Schneeflockenskulpturen, topografischen Marmormodellen von Autobahnkreuzen in Los Angeles, Gemälden, Zeichnungen und Videoarbeiten. Die Ausstellung in der Kunsthalle Bern bildet die bislang umfassendste Präsentation von Sones Werk in Europa.

Diese ehrgeizige Ausstellungsreihe und Publikation wären nicht zustande gekommen ohne die großartige Unterstützung vieler engagierter Menschen.

Die Ausstellung in der Renaissance Society, *Forecast: Snow*, wurde ermöglicht durch die finanzielle Unterstützung der Zell Family Foundation. Als weitere Sponsoren wirkten die Sara Lee Foundation und die Japan Foundation. Der Ausstellungskatalog wurde großzügig gefördert von Bert A. Lies, Jr. und Rosina Lee Yue und unterstützt seitens der W.L.S. Spencer Foundation.

X-Art Show wurde vom Aspen Art Museum organisiert und finanziell gesichert durch Amy und John Phelan sowie durch die Unterstützung des AAM National Council. Für den Katalog haben Bert A. Lies, Jr. und Rosina Lee Yue sowie Vicki und Kent Logan Bürgschaften übernommen. Zusätzliche Unterstützung erhielten wir vom Aspen Magazine.

Die Kunsthalle Bern dankt der Japan Foundation und der Stanley Thomas Johnson Foundation für ihre großzügige Unterstützung, welche diese Ausstellung und den Katalog ermöglicht hat. Ein weiterer Dank geht an die Stadt und den Kanton Bern, sowie die SRG SSR Idée Suisse und den Club 15 für ihr fortwährendes Engagement für das Programm der Kunsthalle.

Die vorliegende Publikation möchte einiges an Hintergrund zu Yutaka Sones bemerkenswertem Werk nachzeichnen. In diesem Zusammenhang sind wir Benjamin Weissman dankbar, der sich immer wieder mit Yutaka Sone auf Ski-Abenteuer-Touren begibt und einen "köstlichen" Text geschrieben hat, der unser Verständnis von Sones spezifischer Mischung aus Fiktion und Realität bereichert. Hamza Walker, Kurator und Leiter der Kunstvermittlung an der Renaissance Society, konzentriert sich in seinem Beitrag auf Sones jüngste Serie von Marmorskulpturen von Schneeflocken, die er im Kontext der Kunst- und Wissenschaftsgeschichte betrachtet anhand ihres Bezugs zu dem Projekt Wilson A. Bentleys, dessen Sammlung von Fotografien einzelner Schneeflocken typisch ist für eine Ära, in der künstlerische und wissenschaftliche Repräsentation mehr gemein hatten.

Unser Dank gilt auch Nina Oeghoede für ihre umsichtige editorische Koordination sowie Kim Beirnaert für ihre einfühlsame Herangehensweise an die grafische Gestaltung dieser Publikation. Ein besonderes Dankeschön geht an Min Nishihara, sowie die Assistenten des Künstlers Sky Burchard, Michael Bauer, Larissa Brantner James and Lauren Mollica. Dank gebührt ausserdem Yutaka Sones Galeristen David Zwirner und seiner Mitarbeiterin Hanna Schouwink für ihr weitreichendes Engagement in diesem Projekt. Schließlich danken wir Yutaka Sone, einem erstaunlichen Künstler, dessen Energie und Enthusiasmus dieses Projekt zu einer fantastischen Reise für uns alle gemacht haben.

Susanne Ghez, Direktorin und leitende Kuratorin,
The Renaissance Society at The University of Chicago

Heidi Zuckerman Jacobson, Direktorin und leitende Kuratorin,
Aspen Art Museum

Philippe Pirotte, Direktor und leitender Kurator,
Kunsthalle Bern

Installation view / Installationsansicht *Forecast: Snow*
The Renaissance Society, 2006

The Phenomenology of Snow

Benjamin Weissman

There was snow falling from the sky every day, tick-tick-ticking against the skiers' windows. They could hear it in their sleep as if the snowflakes were in cahoots with the sandman, lulling the skiers into slumber and steering their dreams toward snow theatre, then gently whispering them awake before dawn, and in the morning the skiers stepped outside to greet the snow and see how much had fallen overnight, and shovel a narrow path to their doors and feel the dry cold crystals mist across their faces. Over the winter there had been speedy, sideways snow, escorted by a strong wind, west to east, loud, deliberate, bossy snow, possibly angry, loading up in freaky drifts. There were snowflakes streaming down, then mysteriously changing direction, what is often recognized as confused snowflake syndrome, where the snowflake in question wanders upwards like a lost balloon and sings a private *woe is me, I am a lonely snowflake* song, and continues its climb back home, cloud bound, while other flakes twirl and loop around it with glee, murmuring an encouraging chorus of *you can't go home again*, which every snowflake knows in its heart. There was big, crumbly, rumble-in-the-jungle snow, and on the slopes there were spines and spires, plumes, flutes and glutes noodling downward with the little oval heads of skiers in shiny helmets and goggles and poofy down jackets steering their arses over rocks and in between trees; there was big, wonky snowflake-snow careening downward, flakes so bloated and drunk that each snowflake had its own bib and barbeque tongs and spatula and parachute and special spotlight and vanity mirror and feather boa; there was silky shiny snow and blue snow like it came from the skim milk god and chocolate chip speckled snow among the rocks. Erased street signage, cabins and lodges submerged into the white meringue, all color removed from the air, and the skiers' eyes operating in dream mode; a demonstrative crow, the great bird of mockery, announces his presence with a few squawks. Everything now, the crow seemed to say, is white or black. A reductive world.

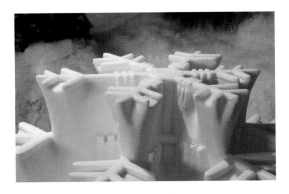

"Every Snowflake has a Different Shape", 2005
Marble/Marmor
54.6 x 80 x 80 cm [21 1/2 x 31 1/2 x 31 1/2 in]

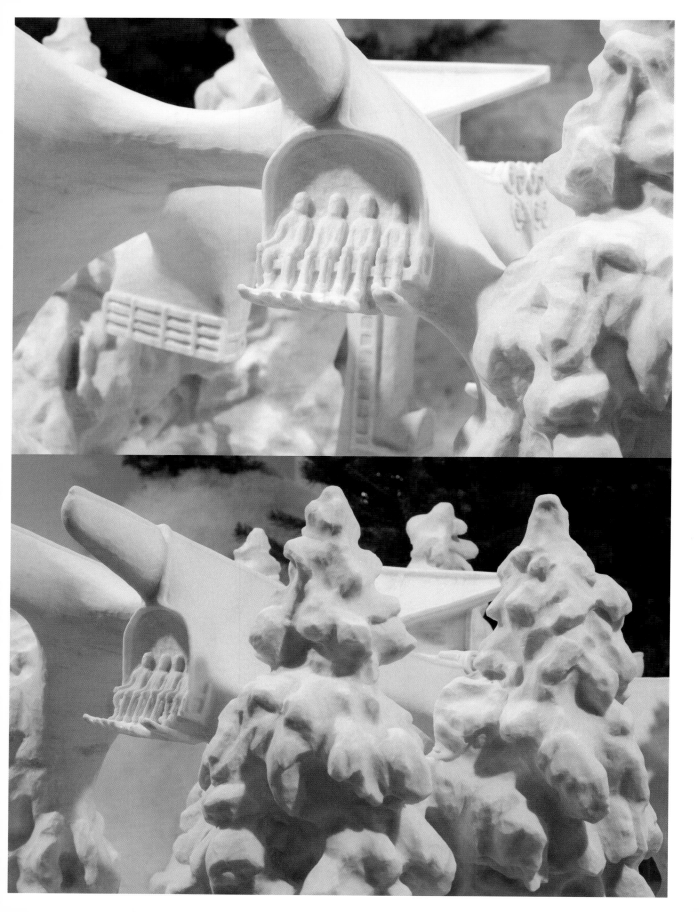

There was squeaky spongy snow on the sidewalks that cooed like pigeons or old ladies when stepped on, chalky snow in the center of flat steep faces that school teachers could use to write on blackboards; there were big breakable chunks of snow that cracked and crumbled like dinner plates; there was manky snow that melted and froze and wished to be left alone, and goose feather snow, and super juicy, pineapple sorbet snow, and snow like a baby's behind, like pudding, pabulum, and creamy cake frosting, and there was snow finer than sugar that got dubbed Suge Knight though much sweeter than Death Row records and it swirled around via the wind, all misty-moody as if caught in a witch's secret tornado, and settled in gullies. There was granulated corn snow and sparkly, iridescent, Ziggy Stardust snow, all gauzy and gossamer that whispered like a dead child with hidden eyes and veils and purple jewels and shiny yellow light and there was harsh, brutal *sastrugi*—a Norwegian word that is fun to pronounce and might mean snow that builds up on windy ridges and shapes itself into strange ice forms of uneven pattern that might look like frozen waves, hard and armor-like, comical and loud to ski over, horrible some might say, still others, fascinating, as their teeth rattled around in their heads, or as one skier named Yutaka would say, we ski it *survival style*.

A cloud descended to 9000 feet and enveloped the skiers, surrounded their brains, and eventually the thick shifting cloud maneuvered inside everything, traveled through trees, in between every pine needle and strand of hair, turning the skiers invisible, only light and dark monochromes, white snow falling, a bright gray sky that seamlessly connected to the earth, and how this turned the world quiet. If there was so much fire and so many pitchforks in hell, heaven was without question wall to wall snow. There was the steel blue air before darkness, when the moon was full, illuminating the

Ski Lift, 2004-2005
Marble/Marmor
80 x 98 x 89 cm [31 1/2 x 38 1/2 x 35 in]

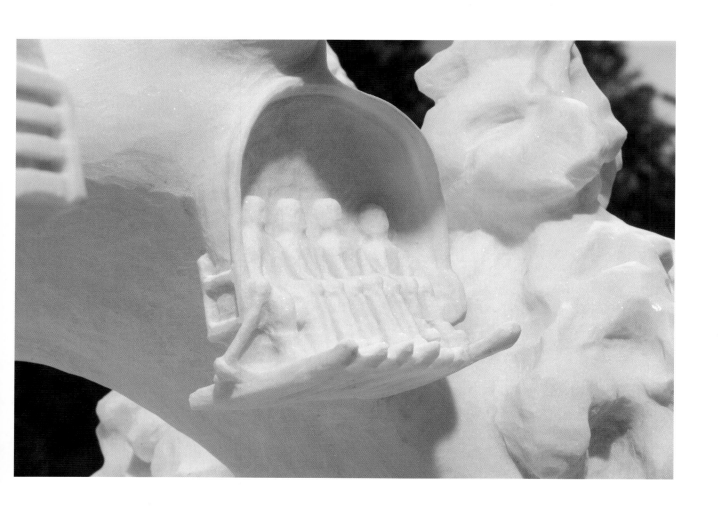

reflecting snowfields with so much light that the skiers didn't have to stop at dusk, they could climb up slopes and read their Robert Walser books on the peaks and ski all night long among the curious cunning coyotes who marveled at their speed. There was the peculiar nausea that struck just before they set out for the day which amounted to discrete gastrointestinal expulsions via the esophagus involving various food groups such as unmasticated Swedish meatballs that journeyed out of the skiers' stomachs and arched out of their mouths like dark humble artillery, just barely making it over the bottom lip, staining the snow a reddish brown, a horrific spectacle to be sure but the skiers reminded each other that they all felt remarkable, less bound to the earth, better able to fly over rocks this way.

When April came and the snow melted, unusual things were revealed in the mountains. There were white mittens, bent ski poles, a large pair of dice, and old bicycles, lens-less glasses, brassieres, teenage underwear, and Hello Kitty slippers. By May the sun finally emerged with true purpose and a rapid thaw occurred; the snow yellowed into a thick gloppy cheese that stopped the skiers like glue. Hey, they all said as their bodies lurched forward on their skis, are you sticking? Yes they were congealed, moving in slow motion and they waxed their skis in the evening but no wax could save them from the mashed potato snow that insisted all skiers slow to a crawl and make snowcones and snowballs and snowfries.

At 10,000 feet where the highest grove of trees resides, in a spot called Scooter Pie, there were small snow-blasted trees bent over from hurricane winds, without a speck of green or brown visible, only white. Underneath the mountain there was running water, talking to itself, trickling and gurgling. And from far away the skiers appeared very small, like tiny unindustrious ants moving about the white gargantuan landscape; closer up, the skiers appeared as if they were dancing by themselves, single file, in a tango line.

The sun continued its spring cleaning and the snow hissed off the steep metal A-frames in voluptuous roofalanches and thumped bluntly to the ground like a pile of white grand pianos. And long second story icicles reached 18 feet and touched bottom. And the towering berms on the street that rose as high as the second story of the cabins took on a melancholic quality and began to compact and droop in the middle, discolored to a shade of opaque fat or the blubber inside a whale.

There were millions of bright red ladybugs clustered all over the snowfields and just before dusk the slumbering upside down bats flew out of their caves and over the fir trees and ate all the ladybugs quite quickly, and weren't they tasty, as well as several dozen XXL dragon flies who were also present in the snow, turning the early evening into a bat protein party with a pink alpenglow that brightened and then dimmed to a light dark. When the skiers saw the bats flying overhead they stopped and watched. Nothing was more beautiful than a black sky full of flapping creatures. Some strays drifted away from the pack and flew close to the skiers. One regular fellow, regular in the gastrointestinal sense, managed to drop a tiny ass load of bat guano onto the tip of a ski. It was like a blessing and the day became even better. The bats returned to their cave, clawed their way to an ideal upside-down position, whereupon a furious orgy ensued. The copulating bats had an aggressive approach to sex and bit each other in a mad hyper panic and then let loose mad pellets of guano. The bats moved briskly across their cave ceiling via their strong pinky claws like kids at recess on a jungle gym.

From a great distance across the mountain the skiers' tracks could be seen: little chicken scratches on the firm snow, loopy figure eights in the pow, curly squiggles, long S shapes, or two straight lines. The skiers each privately wondered about dying in the mountains: would this be the best place for them to live their final days? This thought lead the skiers to try riskier maneuvers, jumping off bigger and bigger rocks, and petite cliff-ettes, but the skiers were landing so gracefully it was as if the mountain waited to catch them. At night the skiers drew pictures and sewed up their torn clothes and played chess, plucked and strummed guitars and sang spontaneous songs about their day together on the mountain, and read more Robert Walser, a writer who died in the snow, with his hand over his heart. They cooked lamb legs and swine loins and sausages and potatoes. When the weather got warm and they could take off their helmets they wore wigs and listened to *Aladdin Sane* and *Hunky Dory* and *Young Americans* and danced on tables. They sprinkled cayenne pepper on their bare feet, or maybe they did that when it was freezing. All at once they were struck by a powerful exhaustion that made their breath slow and their eyes heavy and their limbs twitchy. It was time to sleep and the skiers quickly fell into a deep sleep and they dreamt about the shrine they intended to build in one night on top of the mountain. The shrine would have many flat stones with protective eyes painted at all four corners, a clothes line with big palm fronds and banana leaves, dried pink and yellow poppies, a blue velvet sash, purple seashells, wooden buttons, a much loved stuffed bunny rabbit doll, pictures of snow tigers. Deep inside the shrine there would be a yak butter lantern, a spatula, and a giant crystal snowflake.

A beautiful day (video stills), 2001

Gold Rush, 2005
Acrylic on canvas/Acryl auf Leinwand
45.7 x 61 cm [18 x 24 in]

Gotoma / Dragon Tail, 2006
Acrylic on canvas/Acryl auf Leinwand
61 x 81.3 cm [24 x 32 in]

Apache/Dragon Tail, 2006
Acrylic on canvas/Acryl auf Leinwand
45.7 x 61 cm [18 x 24 in]

Peach Skis and Ski Lift Painting, 2001
Wood, fiber glass, paint and binding, painting/
Holz, Fiberglas, Farbe und Skibindung, Malerei

Die Phänomenologie des Schnees

Benjamin Weissman

Schnee fiel vom Himmel, Tag für Tag, tick-tick-tickend gegen die Fenster der Skiläufer. Sie konnten ihn hören im Schlaf, als wenn der Schnee sich mit dem Sandmann verschworen hätte, die Skifahrer in den Schlummer zu wiegen und ihre Träume ins Schneetheater zu lenken, sie dann sanft wach zu flüstern vor dem Morgengrauen, und am Morgen traten die Skiläufer nach draußen, um den Schnee zu begrüßen und zu sehen, wie viel über Nacht gefallen war, und einen schmalen Pfad frei zu schaufeln zu ihren Türen und zu spüren, wie die trockenen, kalten Kristalle über ihre Gesichter nebelten. Den Winter hindurch war es ein schneller, seitwärts fallender Schnee gewesen, eskortiert von einem starken Wind, von West nach Ost, ein lauter, entschlossener, herumkommandierender Schnee, vielleicht ärgerlich, sich aufhäufend in unvorhersehbarem Treiben. Es gab Schneeflocken, die herabwogten, um dann auf rätselhafte Weise ihre Richtung zu ändern, was allgemein bekannt ist als das verwirrte Schneeflockensyndrom, wenn die besagte Schneeflocke aufwärts weht wie ein verlorener Ballon und ein stilles *wehe mir, ich bin eine einsame Schneeflocke* singt und ihren Anstieg heimwärts fortsetzt, wolkenwärts, während andere Flocken fröhlich zwirbeln und Schleifen drehen, einen beherzten Refrain murmeln von *du kannst nicht wieder nach Hause zurück*, den jede Schneeflocke in ihrem Innersten kennt. Es gab großen, brockigen, rumplig wilden Schnee, und auf den Hängen entstanden Grate, Spitzen, Furchen und Ballungen, sich abwärts schlängelnd mit den kleinen ovalen Köpfen der Skiläufer in glänzenden Helmen und Skibrillen, in affigen Daunenjacken, ihre Ärsche über Felsen und zwischen Bäumen hindurch steuernd; es gab großen, klapprigen Schneeflocken-Schnee, der abwärts torkelte, Flocken so aufgedunsen und betrunken, dass jede Schneeflocke ihre eigene Schürze trug mit Grillzange und Schippchen und Fallschirm und ihren speziellen Scheinwerfer besaß und ihren Schminkspiegel samt Federboa; es gab seidigen glänzenden Schnee und blauen Schnee, als käme er vom Gott der Magermilch, und Stracciatella-gesprenkelten Schnee zwischen den Felsen. Gelöschte Straßenschilder, Hütten und Chalets, eingetaucht in die weiße Meringue, alle Farbe aus der Luft entfernt, und die Augen der Skiläufer arbeiteten im Traummodus; eine demonstrative Krähe, jener große Vogel des Spotts, verkündete seine Gegenwart mit einigen Krächzern. Alles, schien die Krähe zu sagen, ist nun schwarz oder weiß. Eine reduzierte Welt.

   Es gab quietschenden Schwammschnee auf den Gehwegen, der gurrte wie Tauben oder alte Damen, wenn man darauf trat, kreidigen Schnee inmitten von flachen steilen Hängen, den Schullehrer hätten benutzen können, um damit auf Tafeln zu schreiben; es gab große brüchige Klumpen Schnee, die knackten und zerbrachen wie Essensteller; es gab ekelhaften Schnee, der schmolz und überfror und wünschte allein gelassen zu werden, und Gänsefederschnee, und super saftigen Ananas-Sorbet-Schnee, und Schnee wie ein Babypopo, wie Pudding, Pabulum und cremiger Kuchenguss, und es gab Schnee, feiner als Zucker, der den Spitznamen »Suge Knight« bekam, obwohl um vieles süßer als *Death Row* Alben, und er wirbelte über den Wind umher, ganz nebelverhangen gestimmt, als ob er in einem Hexentornado gefangen wäre, und sammelte

Solitude, 2005
Acrylic on canvas / Acryl auf Leinwand
27.9 x 35.6 cm [11 x 14 in]

sich in Schluchten, Rinnen, Felsspalten. Es gab granulierten Mais und funkelnden, schillernden *Ziggy Stardust* Schnee, ganz durchscheinend und hauchfein, der flüsterte wie ein totes Kind mit verborgenen Augen und Schleiern, mit purpurnen Juwelen und glänzendem gelben Licht, und es gab rauen, brutalen *Sastrugi* — ein norwegisches Wort, das sich lustig ausspricht und vielleicht eine Art Schnee bedeutet, der sich an windigen Graten sammelt und zu seltsamen Eisgestalten von krauser Musterung formt, die vielleicht wie gefrorene Wellen aussehen, hart und rüstungsartig, grotesk und schrill zum drüberskiern, grässlich könnten manche sagen, andere faszinierend, wenn ihre Zähne im Kopf herum klappern, oder, wie ein Skiläufer namens Yutaka sagen würde, wir laufen Ski *survival style*.

Eine Wolke stieg herab auf knapp unter 3000 Meter und hüllte die Skiläufer ein, umgab ihre Gehirne, und schließlich fand die dichte wandelnde Wolke einen Weg in alles hinein, wanderte durch Bäume, zwischen jeder Kiefernnadel und jeder Haarsträne, die Skiläufer unsichtbar machend, nur helle und dunkle Monochrome, weißer Schnee fiel, ein leuchtend grauer Himmel, der nahtlos an die Erde anknüpfte, und wie dies der Welt Stille gebot. Wenn es so viel Feuer und Mistgabeln in der Hölle gäbe, dann wäre der Himmel ohne Frage von vorne bis hinten aus Schnee. Es gab diese stahl-blaue Luft vor der Dunkelheit, wenn der Mond voll war und die reflektierenden Schneefelder mit so viel Licht erleuchtete, dass die Skiläufer nicht mit der Abend-dämmerung aufhören mussten, sie konnten Hänge hinaufklettern und ihre Robert Walser Bücher auf den Gipfeln lesen und die ganze Nacht lang skilaufen zwischen den neugierigen schlauen Kojoten, die sich über ihre Geschwindigkeit wunderten. Es gab die eigenartige Übelkeit, die sie überfiel, kurz bevor sie am Morgen aufbrachen, die auf vereinzelte Magen-Darm-Auswürfe über den Ösophagus hinauslief und verschiedene Nahrungsgruppen wie ungekaute schwedische Hackbällchen involvierte, die aus den Mägen der Skiläufer reisten und im Bogen aus ihren Mündern schossen wie dunkle niedere Artillerie, es gerade noch über die Unterlippe schafften und rötlich braune Flecken im Schnee hinterließen, ein entsetzliches Spektakel sicherlich, aber die

Giant Snow Leopard (detail), 2005

Installation view/Installationsansicht *Forecast: Snow*
The Renaissance Society, 2006

Skiläufer erinnerten einander daran, dass sie sich alle erstaunlich fühlten, weniger an die Erde gebunden, auf diese Weise besser in der Lage über Felsen zu fliegen.

Als der April kam und der Schnee schmolz, wurden ungewöhnliche Dinge in den Bergen offenbar. Es gab weiße Fausthandschuhe, verbogene Skistöcke, ein großes Paar Würfel und alte Fahrräder, Brillengestelle, Büstenhalter, Teenager Unterwäsche und Hello Kitty Latschen. Im Mai kam die Sonne endlich mit echter Entschlossenheit heraus, und rascher Tau setzte ein; der Schnee vergilbte zu einem dicken schmatzenden Käse, der die Skiläufer festkleben lies. Hey, sagten sie alle, als ihre Körper auf den Skiern nach vorn ruckten, hängst du fest? Ja, sie waren geronnen, bewegten sich in Zeitlupe, und sie wachsten ihre Skier des Abends, aber kein Wachs konnte sie vor dem Kartoffelbreischnee bewahren, der darauf bestand, dass alle Skiläufer auf Kriechtempo heruntergingen und Schneetüten und Schneebälle und Schneefritten machten.

Auf über 3000 Metern, wo der höchste Hain von Bäumen residiert, an einem Ort namens Scooter Pie, gab es kleine schneegestrahlte Bäume, gebeugt von Wirbelstürmen, ohne dass ein Fleckchen Grün oder Braun sichtbar wären, nur Weiß. Unter dem Berg gab es fließendes Wasser, das mit sich selbst sprach, rieselnd und glucksend. Und von weit weg schienen die Skiläufer sehr klein, wie kleine ungeschäftige Ameisen, die über eine mordsmäßige weiße Landschaft ziehen; von näher dran sahen sie aus, als ob sie für sich selbst tanzten, einzeln in einer Tangoreihe.

Die Sonne fuhr fort mit ihrem Frühjahrsputz, und der Schnee zischte von steilen metallenen A-Rahmen in wollüstigen Dachlawinen und schlug dumpf auf den Boden wie ein Haufen weißer Konzertflügel. Und lange zweigeschossige Eiszapfen erreichten sechs Meter und berührten den Boden. Und die sich auftürmenden geräumten Schneemassen auf der Straße, die bis zum zweiten Stockwerk der Hütten reichten, zeigten sich von ihrer melancholischen Seite und begannen sich zusammenzudrängen

und in der Mitte herunterzuhängen, verfärbt zu einer Schattierung von undurchsichtigem Fett oder Walfischspeck. Es gab Millionen leuchtend roter Marienkäfer, die in Trauben über die Schneefelder verteilt waren, und kurz vor Sonnenuntergang flogen die kopfüber schlummernden Fledermäuse aus ihren Höhlen und über die Tannen und verspeisten ziemlich schnell sämtliche Marienkäfer, und lecker waren sie, so wie mehrere Dutzend XXL Libellen, die ebenfalls im Schnee zugegen waren und den frühen Abend in eine Fledermaus-Protein-Party verwandelten in einem rosaroten Alpenglühen, das erst heller wurde und sich dann zu einer leichten Dunkelheit eintrübte. Als die Skiläufer die Fledermäuse über ihren Köpfen fliegen sahen, hielten sie an und schauten. Nichts war schöner als ein schwarzer

"Every Snowflake has a Different Shape" (detail), 2005
Marble/Marmor
54.6 x 80 x 80 cm [21 1/2 x 31 1/2 x 31 1/2 in]

Himmel voller flatternder Geschöpfe. Einige Querschläger trieben von ihrem Schwarm ab und flogen dicht an den Skiläufern vorbei. Einem normalen kleinen Kerl, normal im verdauungstechnischen Sinn, gelang es, einen winzigen Arsch voll Fledermaus-Guano auf die Spitze eines Skis abzuladen. Es war wie ein Segen, und der Tag wurde noch besser. Die Fledermäuse kehrten in ihre Höhle zurück, kämpften sich zurück in eine ideale kopfüber Position, worauf eine furiose Orgie einsetzte. Die kopulierenden Fledermäuse gingen aggressiv an den Sex heran und bissen einander in einer irren Hyperpanik und schossen dann mit irrem Guano-Schrot. Die Fledermäuse bewegten sich mit ihren starken rosigen Klauen flink über die Decke ihrer Höhle wie Kinder während der Ferien in einem Klettergarten.

Aus großer Entfernung konnte man die Spur der Skiläufer sehen: kleines Hühner-Scharren auf dem festen Schnee, verschlungene Achten im Puder, lockige Krakel, lange S-Formen oder zwei gerade Linien. Jeder für sich machten sich die Skiläufer ihre Gedanken über das Sterben in den Bergen: Wäre dies der beste Ort, ihre letzten Tage zu verleben? Dieser Gedanke brachte die Skiläufer dazu riskantere Manöver auszuprobieren, von immer größeren Felsen zu springen und zierlichen Klippchen, aber die Skiläufer landeten so elegant, es war, als ob der Berg nur darauf wartete, sie aufzufangen. Nachts zeichneten die Skiläufer Bilder und nähten ihre zerrissenen Klamotten und spielten Schach, zupften und klampften auf Gitarren und sangen spontane Lieder über ihren gemeinsamen Tag auf dem Berg, lasen mehr Robert Walser, einen Schriftsteller, der im Schnee starb mit einer Hand auf seinem Herzen. Sie kochten Lammbeine und Schweinelenden und Würstchen und Kartoffeln. Wenn das Wetter wärmer wurde und sie ihre Helme abnehmen konnten, trugen sie Perücken und hörten *Aladdin Sane* und *Hunky Dory* und *Young Americans* und tanzten auf Tischen. Sie streuten Cayenne Pfeffer auf ihre nackten Füße, oder vielleicht war das auch, als es eiskalt war. Urplötzlich überfiel sie alle eine mächtige Müdigkeit, die ihre Atmung langsam, ihre Augen schwer werden und ihre Glieder zucken ließ. Es war Zeit zu schlafen, und die Skiläufer fielen rasch in einen tiefen Schlummer, und sie träumten von dem Schrein, den sie nachts auf einem Gipfel bauen wollten. Der Schrein sollte aus vielen flachen Steinen gemacht werden, mit schützenden Augen, die an alle vier Ecken gemalt wären, einer Wäscheleine mit großen Palmwedeln und Bananen-blättern, getrockneten rosa und gelben Mohnblumen, einer blauen Samtschärpe, pur-purnen Muscheln, Holzknöpfen, einem innig geliebten Stoffhäschen, Bildern von Schneetigern. Tief im Innern des Schreins befänden sich eine Laterne mit Yak-Butter, ein Schippchen und eine gigantische kristalle Schneeflocke.

Chair 14, 2005
Acrylic on canvas / Acryl auf Leinwand
27.9 x 35.6 cm [11 x 14 in]

Camping 1, 2006
Acrylic on canvas / Acryl auf Leinwand
45.7 x 61 cm [18 x 24 in]

Magic Stick, 1999

Installation view/Installationsansicht *IDYL – As to Answer that Picture*
Middelheim Open Air Museum, 2005

Double River Island, 2001
Acrylic on canvas / Acryl auf Leinwand
61 x 121.9 cm [24 x 48 in]

Hong Kong Island (Chinese) (detail), 1998
Marble/Marmor
65 x 120 x 80 cm [25 5/8 x 47 1/4 x 31 1/2 in]

The Time of the Landscape

Philippe Pirotte

Landscape as a fusion of nature and culture, the physical experience of untouched nature (an area so varied it cannot be standardised) and the map are three different things. While travelling extensively during his architectural studies, Yutaka Sone realised "it was impossible to tell what a place really looked like from the map."[1] When does a landscape appear "recognisable" in relation to the map? Which physical place "tallies" with its image or relates to its coded notation? In the past, travellers attempted to chart and translate the experiences and perception of their surroundings within a coded system. Sone's consideration, however, implies a turnabout to this motive. His traveller goes in search of the landscape that correlates to an impression he first gained from the map. He "checks" this out, not from a scientific viewpoint but chiefly from a kind of disbelief. It is a well-known fact that maps invoke dreaming and fantasising about distant places—about departure rather than arrival—and that, paradoxically enough, they still hold a promise of the unknown and of the ever-more-difficult-to-find blank spots. The traveller attempts to construct harmony between the map and reality. This can be an aesthetic experience, not entirely unlike the experiencing of the sublime previously ascribed to landscape perception, intertwined with the fiction of one's own imagination and an interpretive feedback to the map.

Untitled (Double River Island), 2003
Ink, white-out on paper / Tinte, Tipp-Ex auf Papier
21.6 x 27.9 cm [8 1/2 x 11 in]

Highway Junction 405-10 (detail), 2003
Marble/Marmor
22.5 x 118.3 x 161.2 cm [8 7/8 x 46 1/2 x 63 1/2 in]

Much of Sone's work is built up around moments of "recognition", when a place suddenly reveals its relationship to a remarkable, fresh viewpoint. His art allows us to rediscover something we might already know, but have in one way or another failed to recognise and appreciate. To this end, Sone does not reassess old myths, metaphors or allegories associated with experiencing landscape, rather he enhances a renewed understanding of our presence in contemporary landscape. Intensifying and heightening this experience through an exploration of other possible ways of perception, is for Sone a necessary spiritual complement for a mechanised world.

Sone enjoys getting lost in the jungle—at first glance a pure romantic longing. The complexity of the jungle, without physical boundaries but full of creation and change, as a variety of changed directions without a centre, never generates meaning in itself.[2] Free of conventional frameworks and accepted customs, it is always, inevitably, our creative vision which balances the experience of the jungle between absolute meaninglessness and landscape. Sone values the paradox of this experience as one of the major spiritual premises for his artistic undertakings.

In his Los Angeles highway junctions, Sone condenses and transforms the Los Angeles freeway system into almost silky, white marble sculptures of a delicate beauty surrounded by a chaotic jungle setting with living plants. In these "environments with sculpture", jungle and urban schizophrenia are both treated equally, yet absolutely alienated from each other. Despite their amazing accuracy, the sculptures of Los Angeles freeway junctions are somewhat unreal—their tangle of roads, neighbourhoods and commercial buildings forming, according to Sone, "a flower in the city". This layering of different levels of reality is paradigmatic of Sone's work. Using fiction to alter perception, Sone's love for the impossible and paradoxical carries our gaze from snowy mountains to jungles and tropical islands until, via a detour of urban craziness, it self-evidently arrives at snowy jungles and snowmen on the California beach.

The returning of the marble to the landscape in the different topographical sculptures of freeway junctions, Hong Kong island or the surrounding area of the Alpen ski resort of Saint-Moritz is something unique. Sone "unhinges" the historic logic of the marble sculpture, which has been inextricably linked with vertical heroic monuments. Within this logic, a marble sculpture always recalls a commemorative representation. It stands on a specific spot and defines this spot in a symbolic language. Sone's portrayal of Los Angeles emphasises, in greatly reduced scale, the complex fanning out of the freeway as the most significant feature of a community that is defined both geographically and psychologically by the car. The artistic action of hacking into marble implies an exercise which connects it to a car tearing into a bend, as if it were a re-enactment. Out of a material borrowed from the landscape—marble—a new landscape is constructed and implicitly experienced. In the various Highway Junctions and other landscape sculptures like *Snow Leopard Hong Kong Island* or *Giant Snow Leopard*, Sone condenses the complex of architecture and landscape, the cultural and the natural or the built-up and unspoiled. His sculptural ambition is clearly different from the one in which the cultural determines the natural and of which Mount Rushmore can be considered an extreme example. When the writer and artist John Ruskin in the British arts magazine *Modern Painters* considered mountains to be the beginning and end of all natural beauty, or the artist John Spence maintained he would love the Alps if the mountains were not there, both made the landscape subordinate to their egotistical

Giant Snow Leopard (work in progress)
Studio Yutaka Sone Chongwu (China), 2005

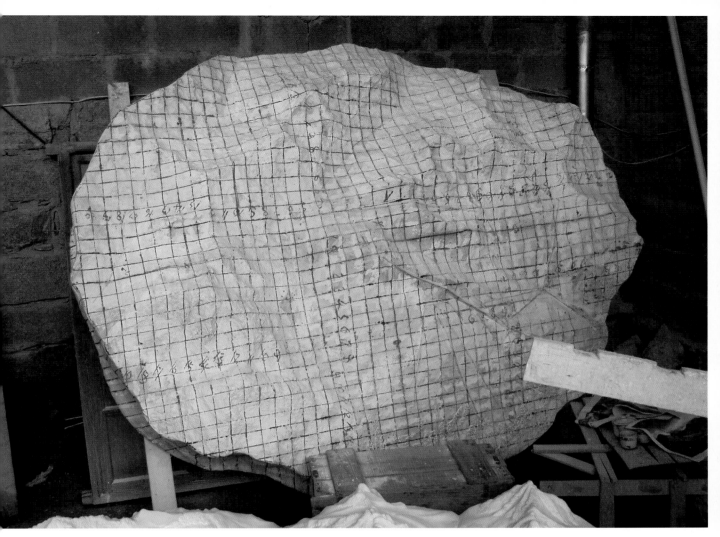

Double River, 2000
Oil on canvas/Öl auf Leinwand
38.1 x 45.7 cm [15 x 18 in]

aesthetic "purpose", as did the sculptor of Mount Rushmore. When Sone makes snow-flakes from natural crystal, carves the Saint-Moritz landscape in white marble or sculpts the Himalayan mountains from snow, we are rather dealing with a strategy of self-denial.

Sone admits he loves landscapes that evoke an intense experience, in which the time of his own presence and that of the landscape exist simultaneously: "I and my time as a human are neither rejected nor accepted, they are not even needed there."[3] Under-lining in his work the experience of such an exalted moment, he crystallises the tension of magical sensations in a person's mediated relationship to his or her environment. It is the experience—after all the jungle cannot venerate itself—that has a "form": a beginning and an end, suddenness, a frame of mind, patterns—meaning. Thus, free-ways, space shuttles, roller coasters, bikes, ski jumps, magic sticks or special gear to move around in a landscape are important to Sone as devices that give form to this relationship. Its limits are defined by the movements these devices induce, like lift-offs, tearing around bends, hurtling down in a roller coaster, climbing mountains or skiing. Sone does not consider the "kick" of exploratory travel, adventure, sport and speed machines from a pessimistic and apocalyptic viewpoint, as one of the necessary stimuli for modern man to compensate for poverty of experience. For him the "kick" is "giving form". Urged by the feeling of the "kick", a kind of delightful shock experience, one gives into things, compelling them to take something of ones own or even forcing them. Consequently, experience as a "kick" has not necessarily separated itself from life and meaning. In Sone's approach the "kick" triggers a physical sense of place and also of time. It provokes no "high", in which one loses oneself in an unreal experience of the world, but is rather a deliberate, almost situationist approach to a reality which seems to be increasingly evicted from its own time and space.

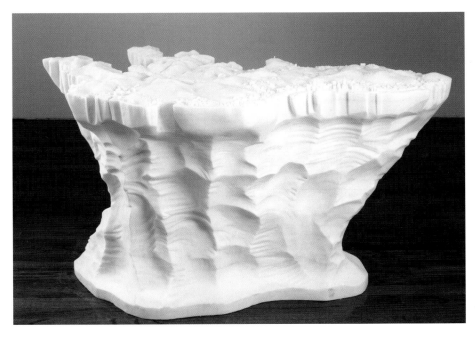

Hong Kong Island (Chinese), 1998
Marble/Marmor
65 x 120 x 80 cm [25 5/8 x 47 1/4 x 31 1/2 in]

Untitled (Double River), (no date)
Acrylic on paper/Acryl auf Papier
35.6 x 50.8 [14 x 20 in]

Time appears to be one of the most important materials for organising the "experience" within Yutaka Sone's projects. An exhibition moment functions only as a fragment within a wider perception of time, yet even within this momentum Sone creates speed-ups, slow-downs and surprises which again transport us to a wilderness of "ahs" and "ohs". For the viewer an exhibition functions as a "hub", a junction in which various perceptions of time come together. Sone links skiing, travelling, trekking in the jungle and organising mega-events to the practice of exhibiting. The time of the exhibition never entirely abstracts itself from the stream of events—among so many other things —happening to the artist. A work of art is not only completed within the aesthetic realm of being "shown", but also within a de-sublimating strategy, which continually displaces the object and underlines non-visual codes, via a shared performative experience or the way in which the artwork is being remembered and recounted. His projects are often incomplete, though not exhibited as pipe dreams or "unrealised projects", they are both finished and can be picked up again. In his own words: "The act of completing an installation is like the act of disrupting a landscape. I might leave my installations incomplete, but intentionally so. Someday I'd like to be able to say that I am something of a landscape." In search of the singularity of the event, Sone chooses not to give history any effect, but by deliberately leaving it incomplete he keeps open an endless potential, much like architecture that is yet-to-be-built.

Untitled (Double River), (no date)
Marker on poster board / Filzstift auf Plakat
55.9 x 71.1 cm [22 x 28 in]

Sone combines travelling with creating as a form of self-development. He conceives his
life and work as a form of self-"Bildung" but describes this as "building romance",
framing his activities within a desire to become an architect "at the end of all the journeys." Here it is evident that the artist does not see time as a sequence. He travels in
different timeframes, speeded-up, slowed-down, in which past, present and future
merge in relation to a postponed time. Travel for Sone is more than simply a vehicle for
the self-realisation of mankind. Time and space overlap each other in a continuous acti-
vated romance with the landscape. His artistic mode, which he sees as a contemporary
version of landscape painting, underpins this romance. He creates real fiction often
combined with events, emphasising the way in which everything is anticipated, recounted
and lodged in the collective imagination rather than the performative aspect. In this
context it is not insignificant that the marble sculpture *Snow Leopard Hong Kong
Island* (1998) was originally planned as a film about the quest for a sculptor able to hew
the entire island of Hong Kong from one single piece of stone. According to Sone,
Snow Leopard Hong Kong Island is "a sculpture about time, as a movie that is not
haunted by the spectre of time." The incredible crystalline and luminous beauty of the
marble sculpture resonates with Sone's quest for this legendary sculptor.

When we link Sone's "building romance" approach with his focus on landscape, it
seems as if we are dealing with an unrelenting criticism of the naivety of the cultural

topos of the idyllic—as a reassuring, untainted setting for a love story—yet at the same time with an exorcising of its unavoidable irony. In his work Sone connects image and narrative as an answer to the idyll, which resides essentially in the image and cannot exist "in" time, yet has to be searched for, tirelessly, time and again. Consequently, for years he has been working on a large landscape project *Perfect Island* or *It Seems Snow Leopard Island*, an island as landscape, a condensing of the landscape without having to take climate zones and geographical conditions into account. *It Seems Snow Leopard Island* only exists beyond the time of man but Yutaka Sone will continue to travel towards it.

1. Yutaka SONE, quoted by Min NISHIHARA, *From Here to There*, in: Min NISHIHARA (ed.) *Yutaka Sone, Travel to Double River Island*, Toyota Municipal Museum of Art, Toyota, Japan, 2002, p. 11
2. Yoko NOSE, *Travel to Double River Island*, in Min NISHIHARA, 2002, p. 117
3. Yutaka SONE, *Statement for Magic Stick*, 1999, in: Min NISHIHARA, 2002, p. 69

Untitled (Double River), 2003
Ballpoint on paper / Kugelschreiber auf Papier
58.4 x 88.9 cm [23 x 35 in]

Green Jungle, 1999
Mixed media / verschiedene Materialien
92 x 132 x 40.6 cm [36 x 52 x 79 in]

Hello Bat (video still), 1998
VHS video tape/VHS Videoband

Die Zeit der Landschaft

Philippe Pirotte

Die Landschaft als Fusion aus Natur und Kultur, die körperliche Erfahrung unberührter Natur (ein so heterogener Bereich, dass er nicht standardisiert werden kann) und die Landkarte sind drei verschiedene Dinge. Auf ausgedehnten Reisen während seines Architekturstudiums hat Yutaka Sone entdeckt, dass »es unmöglich ist zu sagen, wie ein Ort aussieht, wenn man nur auf eine Landkarte blickt.«[1] Wann erscheint eine Landschaft »erkennbar« im Verhältnis zu einer Landkarte? Welcher physische Raum »stimmt« mit seinem Bild überein und steht in Beziehung zu seiner kodierten Notation? Eins versuchten Reisende, die Erfahrungen und Wahrnehmungen des sie Umgebenden in ein kodiertes System zu übersetzen. Sones Überlegung impliziert hingegen eine Verkehrung dieses Motivs. Sein Reisender zieht auf aus der Suche nach einer Landschaft, die mit einem Eindruck korreliert, den er allererst von einer Landkarte gewonnen hat. Er »überprüft« dies nicht von einem wissenschaftlichen Standpunkt aus, sondern im Wesentlichen aus einer Art Ungläubigkeit heraus. Es ist eine wohlbekannte Tatsache, dass Landkarten Träume und Fantasien von entlegenen Orten hervorrufen — eher vom Abreisen als vom Ankommen — und dass sie paradoxerweise immer noch das Versprechen des Unbekannten und der stets schwieriger auffindbaren weissen Flecken beinhalten. Der Reisende bemüht sich, eine Harmonie zwischen Landkarte und Realität herzustellen. Dies kann eine ästhetische Erfahrung sein, der Erfahrung des Sublimen nicht ganz unähnlich, die früher dem Landschaftserlebnis zugeschrieben wurde, verflochten mit der Fiktion der eigenen Einbildungskraft und einer interpretierenden Rückkopplung an die Landkarte.

Ein Großteil von Sones Arbeit wird um Augenblicke der »Erkenntnis« herum aufgebaut, wenn ein Ort plötzlich seine Beziehung zu einem bemerkenswerten, neuartigen Standpunkt enthüllt. Seine Kunst erlaubt uns, etwas wieder zu entdecken, das wir vielleicht schon kannten, aber bei dem es uns auf die eine oder andere Weise nicht gelungen ist, es zu erkennen und zu würdigen. Dafür unternimmt Sone nicht etwa eine Umwertung alter Mythen, Metaphern oder Allegorien, sondern er legt Nachdruck auf ein erneuertes Verständnis unserer Präsenz in der zeitgenössischen Landschaft. Die Intensivierung und Erhöhung dieses Erlebnisses durch das Erforschen anderer möglicher Wahrnehmungsweisen ist für Sone ein notwendiger spiritueller Ausgleich zu einer mechanistischen Weltsicht.

Sone genießt es, sich im Dschungel zu verirren — auf den ersten Blick eine rein romantische Sehnsucht. Die Komplexität des Dschungels — ohne physische Grenzen jedoch voller Schöpfung und Veränderung, eine Variante von Richtungsänderungen ohne Zentrum — generiert aus sich selbst niemals Bedeutung.[2] Frei von konventionellen Begriffsstrukturen und unreflektierten Gewohnheiten ist es immer, unausweichlich, unsere kreative Vision, die die Erfahrung des Dschungels in der Balance von absoluter

Hello Bat (drawing), 1998
Charcoal on paper / Kohle auf Papier

49

Manhattan II and III, 1999
Acrylic on canvas / Acryl auf Leinwand
31.8 x 40.6 cm [12 1/2 x 16 in] — 27.9 x 35.6 cm [11 x 14 in]

Bedeutungslosigkeit und Landschaft hält. Sone schätzt das Paradoxe an dieser Erfahrung als eine der großen spirituellen Prämissen seiner künstlerischen Unternehmungen.

In seinen Autobahnkreuzen aus Los Angeles verdichtet und verwandelt Sone das Autobahnnetz von Los Angeles zu beinahe seidigen, weißen Marmorskulpturen von delikater Schönheit inmitten einer chaotischen Dschungelumgebung mit echten Pflanzen. In diesen »Environments mit Skulptur« werden Dschungel und urbane Schizophrenie als gleichrangig und doch als völlig voneinander entfremdet behandelt. Trotz ihrer überwältigenden Detailgenauigkeit sind die Skulpturen von Autobahnkreuzen in Los Angeles in gewisser Hinsicht irreal — ihr Wirrwarr von Straßen, Wohngegenden und Geschäftsgebäuden bilden, Sone zufolge, »eine Blume in der Stadt«. Diese Schichtung verschiedener Ebenen von Realität ist paradigmatisch für Sones Arbeit. Indem er Fiktion zur Veränderung unserer Wahrnehmung einsetzt, trägt Sones Liebe zum Unmöglichen und Paradoxen unseren Blick von verschneiten Bergen in Urwälder und auf tropische Inseln, bis er über den Umweg des urbanen Wahns wie selbstverständlich bei verschneiten Urwäldern und Schneemännern am Strand von Kalifornien ankommt.

Die Rückkehr des Marmors in die Landschaft in solch unterschiedlichen topografischen Skulpturen wie Autobahnkreuzen, der Insel Hong Kong oder der Umgebung des alpinen Skigebiets von St. Moritz ist etwas Einzigartiges. Sone hebt die historische Logik der Marmorskulptur aus den Angeln, eine Logik, die unauflöslich mit vertikalen heroischen Monumenten verknüpft ist. Im Rahmen dieser Logik erinnert eine Marmorskulptur immer an ein Denkmal. Sie steht auf einem spezifischen Platz und definiert diesen Ort in einer symbolischen Sprache. Sones Porträt von Los Angeles betont auf äußerst reduziertem Maßstab die komplexe Ausfächerung der Autobahn als signifikantem Merkmal einer Gesellschaft, die sowohl geografisch als auch psychologisch durch das Auto definiert wird. Der künstlerische Akt, in den Marmor zu schlagen, impliziert eine Wiederholungsübung, die ihn mit einem Auto verbindet, das in eine Kurve rast. Aus dem Material, dem Marmor, das aus der Landschaft geliehen ist, wird eine neue Landschaft konstruiert und implizit erfahren. In den verschiedenen Highway Junctions und anderen Landschaftsskulpturen wie *Snow Leopard Hong Kong Island* oder *Giant Snow Leopard* verdichtet Sone die Verbindung aus Architektur und Landschaft, Kultur und Natur oder dem Gebauten und dem Unverdorbenen. Seine bildhauerische Ambition unterscheidet sich deutlich von jener Spielart, bei der das Kulturelle das Natürliche determiniert ist und für die Mount Rushmore ein extremes Beispiel darstellt. Als der Schriftsteller und Künstler John Ruskin in der englischen Kunstzeitschrift *Modern Painters* die Berge als Anfang und Ende aller natürlichen Schönheit bezeichnete, oder der Künstler John Spence behauptete, er würde die Alpen lieben, wenn es keine Berge gäbe, ordneten beide die Landschaft auf dieselbe Weise ihren egoistischen ästhetischen »Zwecken« unter wie es der Bildhauer von Mount Rushmore tat. Wenn Sone jedoch Schneeflocken aus natürlichem Kristall macht, die Landschaft um St. Moritz in weißen Marmor haut oder den Himalaja aus Schnee formt, so haben wir es eher mit einer Strategie der Selbstverleugnung zu tun.

Sone bekennt, dass er Landschaften liebt, die ein intensives Erlebnis hervorrufen, in welchem die Zeit der eigenen Gegenwart und diejenige der Landschaft simultan existieren: »Ich und meine Zeit als Mensch werden weder abgelehnt noch angenommen,

Magic Stick, 1998
Acrylic on canvas / Acryl auf Leinwand
38.1 x 45.7 cm [15 x 18 in]

Magic Stick, 1998
Acrylic on canvas / Acryl auf Leinwand
22.2 x 27.3 cm [8 3/4 x 10 3/4 in]

sie sind dort nicht einmal nötig.«[3] Indem er in seiner Arbeit das Erlebnis eines solch exaltierten Augenblicks unterstreicht, kristallisiert er die Spannung von magischen Empfindungen in der mittelbaren Beziehung einer Person zu ihrer oder seiner Umgebung. Es ist das Erleben—schließlich kann der Dschungel sich schwerlich selbst verehren—das eine »Form« hat: einen Anfang und ein Ende, Plötzlichkeit, eine Gemütsverfassung, Muster—Bedeutung. Daher sind Autobahnen, Raumfähren, Achterbahnen, Motorräder, Skischanzen, Zauberstäbe oder Spezialausrüstung, um sich in einer Landschaft umher zu bewegen, wichtig für Sone als Mittel, dieser Beziehung Form zu verleihen. Ihre Grenzen werden definiert von den Bewegungen, die diese Mittel induzieren, wie Raketenstarts, durch Kurven Rasen, in einer Achterbahn Hinabjagen, Bergsteigen oder Skilaufen. Sone betrachtet den »Kick« einer Forschungsreise, von Abenteuer, Sport und Geschwindigkeitsmaschinen nicht von einem pessimistischen und apokalyptischen Standpunkt aus als einen jener Stimuli, die notwendig sind für den modernen Menschen, um die Armut seiner Lebenswelt zu kompensieren. Für ihn besteht der »Kick« in »Formgeben«. Angetrieben von dem Gefühl des »Kicks«, einer Art köstlichen Schockerlebnisses, lässt man Dinge zu und nötigt sie, zwingt sie gar, dadurch etwas von einem selbst anzunehmen. Folglich hat Erleben als »Kick« sich nicht notwendigerweise vom Leben und von der Bedeutung abgetrennt. Bei Sones Herangehensweise löst der »Kick« einen körperlichen Sinn von Ort und auch Zeit aus. Er erzeugt keinen euphorischen Zustand, in dem man sich selbst in einer unwirklichen Erfahrung der Welt verliert, sondern eher einen überlegten, beinahe unmittelbaren Zugang zu einer Realität, die von den Medien in zunehmendem Maß aus der ihr eigenen Zeit und dem ihr eigenen Raum vertrieben zu werden scheint.

Zeit tritt zutage als eines der wichtigsten Elemente für die Organisation des Erlebens in den Projekten Yutaka Sones. Ein Ausstellungsmoment fungiert lediglich als ein Fragment innerhalb einer erweiterten Wahrnehmung von Zeit. Doch selbst in diesem Augenblick schafft Sone Beschleunigungen, Verlangsamungen und Überraschungen, die uns wieder in eine Wildnis aus »Ahs« und »Ohs« versetzen. Für den Betrachter fungiert eine Ausstellung als »Angelpunkt«, ein Verkehrsknoten, an dem unterschiedliche Wahrnehmungen von Zeit zusammentreffen. Sone verknüpft Skilaufen, Reisen, Wandern im Dschungel und das Organisieren von Mega-events mit der Praxis des Ausstellens. Die Zeit der Ausstellung abstrahiert sich selbst nie vollständig vom Strom der Ereignisse, unter so viel ander Dingen—, die dem Künstler widerfahren. Ein Kunstwerk wird nicht nur im ästhetischen Raum des Gezeigtwerdens vollendet, sondern ebenso in einer de-sublimierenden Strategie, die das Objekt ständig verschiebt und die nicht-visuellen Codes unterstreicht mittels einer gemeinsamen performativen Erfahrung oder der Art und Weise, wie ein Kunstwerk erinnert und erzählt wird. Sones Projekte sind häufig unabgeschlossen, ohne deswegen als pure Fantasien oder »nicht realisierte Projekte« ausgestellt zu werden; sie sind gleichermassen beendet und wiederaufgreifbar werden. Er selbst sagt: »Der Akt, eine Installation abzuschließen, ist wie der Akt, in eine Landschaft einzugreifen. Ich lasse meine Installationen vielleicht unvollendet, dies aber absichtlich. Eines Tages würde ich gerne sagen können, dass ich so etwas wie eine Landschaft bin.« Auf der Suche nach der Singularität des Ereignisses entscheidet sich Sone, der Geschichte keinen Effekt zu verleihen, sondern sie absichtlich unabgeschlossen zu lassen und so ein unendliches Potenzial offenzulassen —vergleichbar mit Architektur, die erst noch gebaut werden muss.

Installation view / Installationsansicht Amusement Romana
Toyota Municipal Museum of Art, 2002

Himalayan Mountains, 1999
Acrylic on canvas / Acryl auf Leinwand
45.7 x 55.9 cm [18 x 22 in]

Sone kombiniert das Reisen mit dem Schaffen als einer Form der eigenen Entwicklung. Er versteht sein Leben und Werk als selbst-»Bildung« im klassischen Sinn, beschreibt dies jedoch als »building romance« und fasst damit seine Aktivitäten unter den Wunsch, Architekt zu werden »am Ende all der Reisen«. Hier wird offensichtlich, dass der Künstler Zeit nicht als Sequenz ansieht. Er bereist verschiedene Zeitrahmen, beschleunigt, verlangsamt, in denen Vergangenheit, Gegenwart und Zukunft verschmelzen mit Bezug auf ein Noch-nicht. Reisen bedeutet für Sone mehr als einfach nur ein Vehikel zur Selbstverwirklichung für die Menschheit. Zeit und Raum überlappen einander in einer andauernden, aktiv betriebenen Leidenschaft für die Landschaft. Seine künstlerische Arbeitsweise, die er als zeitgenössische Version der Landschaftsmalerei betrachtet, unterstützt diese Leidenschaft. Er schafft reale Fiktion, oftmals kombiniert mit Ereignissen und betont damit, wie alles vorweggenommen, erinnert und verstaut wird in der kollektiven Vorstellung, und legt so weniger Gewicht auf den performativen Aspekt. In diesem Zusammenhang ist es nicht ohne Bedeutung, dass die Marmorskulptur *Snow Leopard Hong Kong Island* (1998) ursprünglich als Film über die Suche nach einem Bildhauer geplant war, der in der Lage wäre, die gesamte Insel Hong Kong aus einem einzigen Stück Stein zu hauen. Sone zufolge ist *Snow Leopard Hong Kong Island* »eine Skulptur, die von Zeit handelt, wie ein Film, der nicht vom Gespenst der Zeit heimgesucht wird«. Aus der unglaublichen kristallinen und luminosen Schönheit der Marmorskulptur spricht Sones Suche nach diesem legendären Bildhauer.

Installation view/Installationsansicht Jungle Island
Los Angeles Museum of Contemporary Art, 2003

Untitled, 1999
Acrylic on canvas / Acryl auf Leinwand
53.3 x 65.4 cm [21 x 25 3/4 in]

Wenn wir Sones Vorgehensweise (von »building romance«) mit seinem Interesse an Landschaft verbinden, scheint es, als hätten wir es mit einem unnachgiebigen Kritisieren der Naivität des kulturellen Topos der Idylle — als beruhigendem, unverdorbenem Ort einer Liebesgeschichte — zu tun, und doch zugleich mit einer Austreibung der damit unvermeidlich einhergehenden Ironie. In seinem Werk verknüpft Sone Bild und Erzählung zu einer Antwort auf die Idylle, die wesentlich im Bild ansässig ist und nicht »in« der Zeit existieren kann, die aber doch angestrebt werden muss, unermüdlich, wieder und wieder. Konsequenterweise ist er seit Jahren mit einem großen Landschaftsprojekt beschäftigt, *Perfect Island* oder *It Seems Snow Leopard Island*, einer Insel als Landschaft, eine Verdichtung der Landschaft ohne Berücksichtigung von Klimazonen und geografischen Bedingungen. *It Seems Snow Leopard Island* existiert nur jenseits der Menschlichen Zeit, aber Yutaka Sone wird weiterhin unterwegs dorthin sein.

1. Yutaka SONE, zitiert nach Min NISHIHARA, *From Here to There*, in: Min NISHIHARA (Hrsg.), *Yutaka Sone, Travel to Double River Island*, Toyota Municipal Museum of Art, Toyota (Japan) 2002, S. 11
2. Yoko NOSE, *Travel to Double River Island*, in: Min NISHIHARA, 2002, S. 117
3. Yutaka SONE, *Statement for Magic Stick*, 1999, in: Min NISHIHARA, 2002, S. 69

It Seems Snow Leopard Island (work in progress)
Studio Yutaka Sone, South Pasadena, CA, 2006

Palm Tree Head, 2005

Acrylic on canvas/Acryl auf Leinwand
63,5 x 63,5 x 1,3 cm [25 x 25 x $^{1/5}$ in]

Untitled (Double River Island), 2004
Acrylic on paper mounted on plywood / Acryl auf Papier auf Sperrholz
76.2 x 121.9 x 6 cm [30 x 48 x ¹/⁴ in]

Snow Jungle (With Love), 1999
Oil on canvas/Öl auf Leinwand
130.8 x 161.3 cm [51 1/2 x 63 1/2 in]

Highway Junction 14-5, 2002

Marble and plants / Marmor und Pflanzen
34 x 113 x 123.5 cm [13 3/8 x 44 1/2 x 48 5/8 in]

"Every Snowflake has a different Shape", 2005
Graphite, charcoal on paper / Graphit, Kohle auf Papier
55.9 x 66.4 cm [22 x 26.1 in]

Cold Play

Hamza Walker

How full of the creative genius is the air in which these are generated! I should hardly admire more if real stars fell and lodged on my coat. Nature is full of genius, full of the divinity, so that not a snowflake escapes its fashioning hand.

> Henry David Thoreau
> *journal entry*, January 5, 1856

With a structure whose geometry appears to speak confidently of purpose and intent, the snowflake will forever beg the question, who makes these things? As Thoreau's journal entry makes clear, inside every snowflake is the proto-language of Intelligent Design. Over the centuries, the snowflake has been read as the means through which the divine reveals itself, taking exquisite care with something as seemingly infinite in number and variation as it is ephemeral. Its beauty aside, the snowflake remains a fundamental metaphor for the complexity and transience of all living things. Just as soon as the snowflake impresses upon us the idea of a kaleidoscopic order whose harmony is derived through the union of sameness and difference, where one is seen through the other, the snowflake disappears, becoming a sign for that which is in fact elusive.

Proof of the snowflake's infinite variety was borne out after the camera's invention. We owe the certainty with which we are taught "no two snowflakes are alike" to Wilson A. Bentley (1865-1931), a Vermont farmer whose interest in meteorology led him to photograph more than 5,000 snow crystals. These, along with copious notes about the atmospheric conditions when the photos were taken, form a genuine scientific study.

But under Bentley's aegis the subject of awe became the victim of inventory. Each page of *Snow Crystals*, Bentley's two hundred page magnum opus, features twelve hexagonal snowflakes, all of equal size, arranged in grid formation on a black background. Stripped of sentimentality, they amount to the *ne plus ultra* of modernisms, namely an archive. Bentley's singular obsession was beyond doubt a labor of love. As a visual document, it is the culmination of a cultural discourse while being extensive enough to fulfill the scientific imperative of objectivity. Bentley's photographs present the snowflake as a work of art that the camera only serves to reveal as such. His efforts made the snowflake a part of popular consciousness to the extent that it became a definitive staple of kitsch, placing it outside the purview of the fine arts as a subject to be taken seriously.

If the snowflake is any indication, then the natural world is indeed susceptible to cultural fatigue. Representations of flora, fauna and meteorological phenomena belong as much to popular culture as they ever did to fine art. Over the course of modernity, as kitsch lay claim to nature in an uncritical fashion, the fine arts would engage with a metaphysical questioning of our place within and relationship to nature such that the emphasis was as likely to fall on alienation and loss rather than harmony. Caught between kitsch and the fine arts, the singing of nature's praises would become hopelessly

Untitled, 2003
Acrylic on canvas/Acryl auf Leinwand
45.7 x 61 x 2.2 cm [18 x 24 x 0.9 in]

Untitled, 2005
Acrylic on canvas/Acryl auf Leinwand
76.2 x 61 x 4.4 cm [30 x 24 x 1 1/3 in]

susceptible to irony. The most impressive feat of *Forecast: Snow*, Yutaka Sone's paen to the snowflake, is the annulment of any dialectical tension between kitsch and the fine arts, which, four decades after the advent of Pop Art, is as it should be.

A mixed media extravaganza, it features paintings, drawings, sculpture, and last but not least, a forest of roughly 100 pine trees. *Forecast: Snow* mixes contradictory modes of sculptural practices in a manner so playful as to banish any sense of redemption from the immediate horizon. Nestled within what was a winter wonderland were a series of crystal and marble snowflake sculptures ranging from several inches to a few feet in diameter. Sone is interested in a range of idyllic associations with snow, be they dramatic mountainous landscapes such as that surrounding Saint-Moritz, or activities as homespun and humble as making a snow man. A pair of handmade skis and a charming vignette of a wintery ski lift scene hewn in marble reveal Sone's tribute as that of an unabashed thrill seeker. For Sone, the simple pleasures offered by the great snowy outdoors are a source of nature's inexhaustible spiritual currency despite an ever-burgeoning recreation industry. Fully aware of Bentley's project, Sone built his own portable apparatus for photographing hundreds of snowflakes. Thanks to the advent of digital photography, Sone was able to capture snowflakes from a vantage point that exposes Bentley's photographs as relatively clinical. Sone uses a depth of field that, while blurring the background, monumentalizes the snowflake, making it sculptural if not downright architectural. The results are dreamy and romantic enough to qualify as a genuine return to the Pictorialists.

Sone's work is anything but medium specific. Painting, photography, video, performance and sculpture are present throughout his oeuvre in equal measure. For the past three years they have all been put at the service of themes inspired by snow. This includes his stint as the frontman for his rock-n-roll outfit, *The Snowflake Band*, which was memorialized in an artist book produced in conjunction with The Society's portion of the exhibition. Sone's work is entertaining in the performative sense. In 1993, Sone gained international notoriety for *Her 19th Foot*, a performance/sculpture featuring a string of modified bicycles hitched together so as to accommodate 19 riders. Since 1996 he has worked with craftsmen in China to create a striking body of marble sculptures whose subjects have included the island of Hong Kong, roller coasters, and Los Angeles freeway interchanges. Marble is synonymous with sculpture in its honor/memorial guise. Using Sone's marble freeways as a terminus, one could narrate the history of Western Civilization through carved marble statuary, from its cradle in Greece to Los Angeles taken to be its current gravesite.

Not only is marble a standard bearer of the fine arts, it imparts nobility to its subject. Marble's opacity and density make it a geological metaphor for purity and eternity. Subject matter carved in marble is no longer of its present; it belongs to the Ages. Paradoxically, Sone's marble roller coasters and expressway interchanges privilege the momentary over the timeless, motion over stasis. They are sites where the thrill and hustle of contemporary life at their most extreme yet quotidian achieve expression in the form of the arabesque. More subtle but just as intriguing is his marble sculpture *Snow Leopard Hong Kong Island*. Executed in 1997, the year the island reverted to Chinese rule after its 99-year lease to Britain expired, *Snow Leopard Hong Kong Island* is less a monument to the place and more a monument to historic political change. Ultimately Sone's marble works are monuments of and to the present, allowing us to see ourselves in flattering archaeological terms as a civilization that cherishes living in the moment, whether that moment is of historic proportion or as fleeting as the life of a snow flake.

The previous century, however, was noted for having adopted installation-based practices, and industrial materials and methods of fabrication as a direct challenge to two of sculpture's pre-modern paradigms: the artisanal handling of noble materials, and the breathing of life into inert matter. Although we are two generations removed from minimalism, resuscitation of either sculptural paradigm still seems a conspicuous indulgence. For Sone to render in marble a subject taken as proof of God's handiwork, albeit one reduced to kitsch, is to consciously pit a bankrupt form against an equally bankrupt content. The result is that both the marble object and its trivial subject matter are redeemed as guilt-free pleasures. This not to mention their placement within a setting/environment meant to radically expand and therefore challenge the conservative experience of viewing pedestal-based sculpture.

As archeological monuments to a present we are loath to recognize, let alone celebrate, the humor in Sone's work comes at the price of critique framed in terms of loss. Sone's work, no matter how much it revels in bankruptcy, is resistant to mourning, and as a result is immune to irony. It is straight-up fun, delightful even, no strings attached. Monumentalizing the snowflake in the wake of Bentley's archive is perhaps the only way to properly acknowledge the snowflake's fate as kitsch, and at the same time to rescue it from Chapter 11 so that we may once again partake of what have been frozen assets indeed.

Untitled, 2005
Gelatin silver print / Silbergelatinepapier

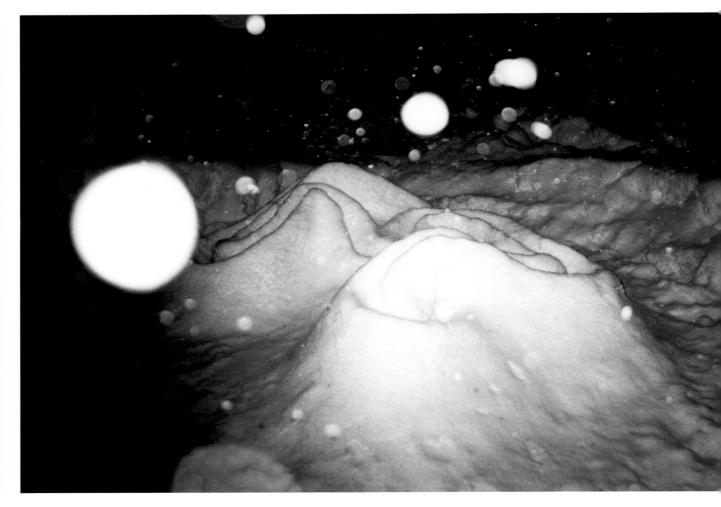

Snow Sculpture (Nagano), 1999
Snow/Schnee

Untitled, 2004
Acrylic on canvas/Acryl auf Leinwand
45.7 x 61 x 2.2 cm [18 x 24 x ⁷/₈ in]

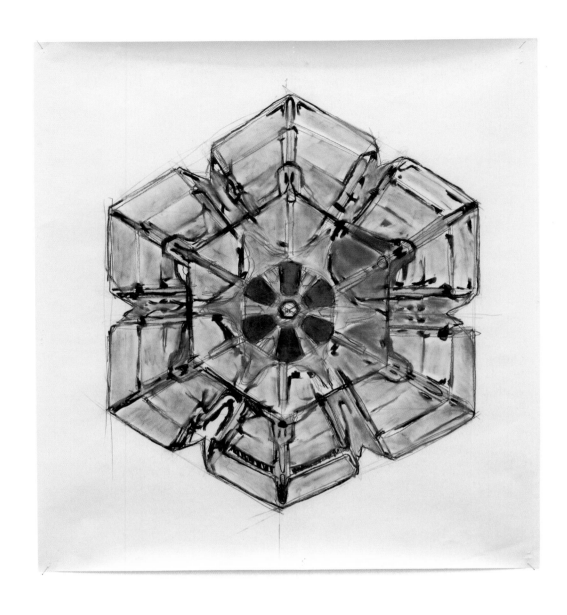

"Every Snowflake has a different Shape", 2005
charcoal on paper/Kohle auf Papier
109.2 x 106.7 cm [43 x 42 in]

"Every Snowflake has a different Shape", 2005-2006
Drawings, mixed media on paper/Zeichnungen, verschiedene Materialien auf Papier
Variable dimensions/Variable Dimensionen

Installation view/Installationsansicht *Forecast: Snow*
The Renaissance Society, 2006

Kaltes Spiel

Hamza Walker

Wie voll des kreativen Geistes ist die Luft, in der diese hervorgebracht werden!
Ich würde es kaum mehr bewundern, wenn echte Sterne fielen und auf meinem
Mantel liegen blieben. Die Natur ist voll von Genie, voll Göttlichkeit, so dass nicht
eine Schneeflocke ihrer modellierenden Hand entkommt.

    Henry David Thoreau
    Tagebucheintrag, 5. Januar 1856

Aufgrund ihrer Struktur, deren Geometrie vertrauensvoll von Ziel und Zweck zu
sprechen scheint, wird die Schneeflocke immer wieder die Frage aufwerfen: Wer macht
diese Dinge? Thoreaus Tagebucheintrag lässt deutlich werden, dass im Innern jeder
Schneeflocke die Proto-Sprache des Intelligent Design angelegt ist. Über die Jahr-
hunderte ist die Schneeflocke als Mittel interpretiert worden, durch das sich das
Göttliche offenbart, indem es solch erlesene Sorgfalt anwendet auf etwas, das solcher-
massen von scheinbar unendlicher Menge und Variation wie ephemer ist. Abgesehen
von ihrer Schönheit ist die Schneeflocke eine grundlegende Metapher für die
Komplexität und die Vergänglichkeit aller Lebewesen. Sobald die Schneeflocke uns
die Vorstellung einer kaleidoskopischen Ordnung nahe legt, deren Harmonie abgeleitet
ist aus der Synthese von Gleichheit und Verschiedenheit, worin das eine durch das
andere gesehen wird, verschwindet die Schneeflocke und wird zu einem Zeichen für
etwas, das sich tatsächlich der Beschreibung, der Erklärung entzieht.

"Every Snowflake has a Different Shape", 2005
Crystal/Kristall
26 x 50 x 51 cm [10 1/4 x 19 3/4 x 20 in]

Der Nachweis der unendlichen Vielfalt der Schneeflocke wurde mit der Erfindung der Fotografie erbracht. Wir verdanken die Gewissheit, mit der wir lernen, dass »keine zwei Schneeflocken gleich sind«, Wilson A. Bentley (1865-1931), einem Bauern aus dem US Bundesstaat Vermont. Sein Interesse an Meteorologie führte ihn dazu, mehr als 5000 Schneekristalle zu fotografieren. Diese Fotografien zusammen mit umfangreichen Beschreibungen der atmosphärischen Bedingungen, unter denen sie aufgenommen wurden, bilden zweifellos eine wissenschaftliche Studie.

Allerdings wurde unter Bentleys Ägide aus einem Ehrfurcht gebietenden Thema ein Opfer des Inventarisierens. Jede Seite von *Snow Crystals* (Schneekristalle), Bentleys zweihundert Seiten starkem Magnum Opus, zeigt zwölf hexagonale Schneeflocken, alle von gleicher Größe, die in einem Raster vor einem schwarzen Hintergrund angeordnet sind. Jeglicher Sentimentalität entkleidet, ergeben sie nicht mehr und nicht weniger als das non plus ultra der Modernismen, nämlich ein Archiv. Bentleys einzigartige Obsession war ohne jeden Zweifel ein Werk der Liebe. Als visuelles Dokument ist es die Kulmination eines kulturellen Diskurses. Gleichzeitig ist es aber hinreichend extensiv und erfüllt so den wissenschaftlichen Anspruch auf Objektivität. Bentleys Fotografien zeigen die Schneeflocke als Kunstwerk; die Kamera dient nur dazu, es als solches zum Vorschein zu bringen. Bentleys Anstrengungen machten die Schneeflocke in einem solchen Maß zu einem Teil des öffentlichen Bewusstseins, dass sie zu einem Inbild von Kitsch verkam und derart außerhalb der Sphäre der schönen Künste platziert als Thema nicht mehr länger ernst genommen wurde.

Wenn die Schneeflocke in dieser Hinsicht aussagekräftig ist, dann ist die Welt in der Tat von einer Kulturmüdigkeit ergriffen worden. Darstellungen von Flora, Fauna und meteorologischen Phänomenen gehören ebenso zur Populärkultur wie sie immer auch zur Kunst gehört haben. Im Laufe der Moderne, als der Kitsch die Natur mit

"Every Snowflake has a Different Shape" no. 19, 2005
Crystal/Kristall
15.5 x 15.5 x 18.5 cm [6 x 6 x 7 1/4 in]

"Every Snowflake has a Different Shape" no. 21, 20
Crystal/Krist.
15.5 x 15.5 x 15 cm [6 x 6 x 5.91

unkritischem Beschlag belegte, setzten sich die Künste mit metaphysischen Fragen bezüglich unseres Platzes innerhalb der Natur und unseres Verhältnisses ihr gegenüber auseinander auf eine Art, die es näher legte, die Entfremdung und den Verlust zu betonen als die Harmonie. Gefangen zwischen Kitsch und der hohen Kunst, wurde das Loblied auf die Natur unweigerlich der Ironie ausgeliefert.

Die beeindruckendste Leistung von *Forecast: Snow*, Yutaka Sones Päan auf die Schneeflocke, ist die Ausklammerung jeglicher dialektischer Spannung zwischen Kitsch und hoher Kunst. Vierzig Jahre nach der Ankunft der Pop Art sollte man meinen, dass dies selbstverständlich wäre. Die Ausstellung ist ein mixed media Feuerwerk mit Gemälden, Zeichnungen, Skulpturen und — last but not least — einem Wald aus ungefähr 100 Kiefern. *Forecast: Snow* mischt widersprüchliche Modi plastischer Praxis auf eine Weise, die so spielerisch ist, dass jeglicher Anklang von Erlösung aus dem unmittelbaren Horizont gebannt ist. In eine wunderbare Winterlandschaft wurde eine Reihe unterschiedlich großer Skulpturen eingebettet, die einen Durchmesser von einigen Zentimetern bis hin zu einem Meter aufweisen. Sone interessiert sich für den gesamten Spielraum der idyllischen Assoziationen, den Schnee weckt, seien es dramatische Berglandschaften wie die Umgebung von St. Moritz oder so schlichte und bescheidene Aktivitäten wie das Bauen eines Schneemanns. Ein paar handgemachter Skier und eine bezaubernde Vignette einer winterlichen Skilift-Szene, die in Marmor geschlagen wurde, lassen Sones Hommage als den Ausdruck von jemandem erscheinen, der ganz unverhohlen nach Nervenkitzel sucht. Für Sone sind die einfachen Freuden, die der Schnee zu bieten hat, ein Quell der unerschöpflichen spirituellen Ströme der Natur, der ständig weiter wuchernden Freizeitindustrie zum Trotz. Sone war sich Bentleys Projekt sehr wohl bewusst, als er seinen eigenen tragbaren Apparat baute, um hunderte von Schneeflocken zu fotografieren. Die digitale

Paper and Plastic Snowballs, 2005
Paper and plastic / Papier und Plastik
86.4 x 86.4 x 50.8 cm [34 x 34 x 20 in]

Fotografie ermöglichte es Sone, aus einer Perspektive zu fotografieren, die Bentleys Aufnahmen als relativ klinisch entlarvt. Sone verwendet eine Tiefenschärfe, die den Hintergrund unscharf, die Schneeflocken monumental, plastisch, wenn nicht gar architektonisch erscheinen lässt. Die Resultate sind so verträumt und romantisch, dass man sie als eine genuine Rückkehr zu den Piktorialisten werten kann.

Sones Arbeit ist alles andere als spezifisch auf ein Medium ausgerichtet. Malerei, Fotografie, Video, Performance, Skulptur sind in seinem Œuvre durchgängig gleichmäßig vertreten. Während der letzten drei Jahre wurden sie alle in den Dienst durch Schnee inspirierte Themen gestellt. So auch sein Auftritt als Frontman seiner Rock-n-roll Gruppe, *The Snowflake Band*, der sich in einem Künstlerbuch niedergeschlagen hat, das in Verbindung mit jenem Teil der Ausstellung hergestellt wurde, für den Renaissance Society verantwortlich zeichnete. Sones Arbeit ist unterhaltsam im performativen Sinn des Wortes. 1993 erlangte Sone internationale Berühmtheit mit *Her 19th Foot*, einer Performance/Skulptur aus einer Reihe umgebauter Fahrräder, die so aneinander gekoppelt wurden, dass sie 19 Fahrern Platz boten. Seit 1996 arbeitet er mit Handwerkern in China an einem erstaunlichen Corpus von Marmorskulpturen, der solche Themen wie die Insel Hong Kong, Achterbahnen und Autobahnkreuze in Los Angeles einschließt. Marmor ist ein Synonym für Skulptur in der Form von Denkmälern und Mahnmalen. Verwendet man Sones marmorne Autobahnen als Terminus, so lässt sich die Geschichte der westlichen Zivilisation anhand der Marmorplastik erzählen, von ihrer Wiege in Griechenland bis hin zu Los Angeles als ihrer angeblichen gegenwärtigen Grabstätte.

Marmor ist nicht nur ein Bannerträger der hohen Kunst, er verleiht seinem Gegenstand auch Noblesse. Seine Undurchsichtigkeit und Dichte machen Marmor zu einer geologischen Metapher für Reinheit und Ewigkeit. Ein Gegenstand, der in Marmor gehauen wurde, gehört nicht länger der Gegenwart an; er besteht für alle Zeit. Paradoxerweise geben Sones marmorne Achterbahnen und Autobahnkreuze dem Momentanen den Vorzug gegenüber dem Zeitlosen, ziehen die Bewegung dem Stillstand vor. Es sind Stätten, an denen der Nervenkitzel und die Hast des gegenwärtigen Lebens extrem und alltäglich zugleich einen Ausdruck der Arabeske erreichen. Subtiler, doch ebenso faszinierend ist seine Marmorskulptur *Snow Leopard Hong Kong Island* von 1997. In jenem Jahr kehrte die Insel zurück unter die Herrschaft des chinesischen Festlands, nachdem die 99-jährige Pacht an die britische Krone ausgelaufen war. *Snow Leopard Hong Kong Island* ist weniger ein Monument für den Ort als ein Monument des historisch-politischen Wandels. Letztendlich sind Sones Marmorarbeiten Monumente der und Monumente für die Gegenwart, die uns erlauben, uns selbst in schmeichlerischen archäologischen Begriffen als eine Zivilisation zu sehen, die das Leben im Augenblick zu würdigen weiß, sei nun dieser Moment von historischer Bedeutung oder aber so flüchtig wie die Lebensspanne einer Schneeflocke.

Das Besondere am vorigen Jahrhundert war allerdings die Einführung von auf der Installation basierten Arbeitsweisen sowie die Verwendung von industriellen Materialien und Fertigungsweisen als direkte Konfrontation zweier vor-moderner Paradigmen der Skulptur: der kunsthandwerkliche Umgang mit edlen Materialien und das Einhauchen von Leben in die träge Materie. Obwohl uns zwei Generationen vom Minimalismus trennen, erscheint die Neubelebung auch nur eines dieser beiden Paradigmen immer noch als ein auffälliger Luxus. Wenn Sone eine Thematik in Marmor ausführt, die als Nachweis göttlichen Handwerks angesehen wird, und sei es auch nur eine, die zum Kitsch reduziert worden ist, so bedeutet das, eine bankrotte Form bewusst einem gleichermaßen bankrotten Inhalt gegenüberzustellen. Das Ergebnis besteht darin, dass sowohl das Marmorobjekt als auch sein triviales Thema wieder zu einem Vergnügen gemacht werden, das von jeglichem Schuldkomplex befreit ist. Ganz zu schweigen von einer Verortung innerhalb einer Aufstellung-cum-Umgebung, welche beabsichtigt, die konservative Erfahrung einer Betrachtung der auf einem Sockel platzierten Skulptur radikal zu erweitern und damit in Frage zu stellen.

Als archäologische Monumente für eine Gegenwart, die wir nur ungern anerkennen, geschweige denn feiern, bezahlt Sones Humor den Preis einer Kritik in der Münze des Verlusts. Seine Arbeit ist gefeit gegen Trauer, so sehr sie sich auch im Bankrott wälzt, und ist daher immun gegen Ironie. Sie ist einfach Spaß, entzückend sogar, ohne Verpflichtungen. Die Schneeflocke im Sinne von Bentleys Archiv zu monumentalisieren, ist vielleicht die einzige Art und Weise, das Schicksal der Schneeflocke als Kitsch angemessen zu würdigen, und sie zugleich vor der Insolvenz unter »Chapter 11« zu retten, so dass wir abermals an etwas teilhaben dürfen, das buchstäblich eingefrorene Vermögenswerte gewesen sind.

"Every Snowflake has a Different Shape" no. 20, 2005
Crystal/Kristall
15.5 x 15.5 x 16 cm [6 x 6 x 6.3 in]

"Every Snowflake has a Different Shape", 2005
Crystal/Kristall
26 x 50 x 51 cm [10 1/4 x 19 3/4 x 20 in]

Beach Project, 2001

Snowflake is going to NY, 2003
Acrylic on canvas / Acryl auf Leinwand
76.2 x 101.6 x 2.2 cm [30 x 40 x ⁷/₈ in]

Having Fun with Yutaka Sone

Heidi Zuckerman Jacobson

Yutaka Sone's practice is whimsical. He paints, draws, performs, and makes sculpture and installations. His ideas bubble up with passion and inspiration. He has virtually no filter, a trait that is endearing and inherently leads to collaboration. He wants everyone to be part of the process, including the sushi chef he met the night before a big day of filming a hike and skiing trip at Aspen's infamous Highland Bowl. The chef joined Sone, filmmaker Damon McCarthy, writer Benjamin Weissman, Aspen Art Museum Facilities and Special Projects Manager Patrick Storey, Buttermilk Mountain Manager Hans Hohl, and artist Peter Doig, who was in town working on a project for the Aspen Art Museum. The eclecticism of what served as the artist's posse for the day is typical and totally "X".

Sone's Aspen Art Museum exhibition, *X-Art Show*, draws its title from the X-Games, the extreme sporting competition that takes place at Buttermilk Mountain in Aspen each winter. The athletes are known for performing seemingly impossible feats on skis, snowboards, motorcycles, and snowmobiles; the greater the apparent danger to the participants, the larger the thrill. Sone likes the idea of all things "X" and the notion that art, in particular his, can be labeled as such. The X-ness relates to Sone's artistic practice as well as its style: fresh, free, and extremely charged.

As part of his larger practice, thrice before Sone has constructed enormous pairs of dice and witnessed them being rolled: onto the desert outside of San Antonio, Texas; at the opening of the 2000 World Exposition in Hannover, Germany; and down the steps of the iconic Opera House in Sydney, Australia. A long-term dream had been to see them tossed down a snowy mountain. (An earlier project in Switzerland never materialized.)

Sone's dice projects involve chance, mysticism, and transcendence in daily life. In Aspen, for a performance titled *Mt. 66*, a pair of newly commissioned, artist-designed, eight-foot-cubed dice was transported by flatbed truck through town, from the Aspen Art Museum, along Main Street, to Buttermilk Mountain, and tossed down the X Games SuperPipe, a giant half-pipe. Inspired by Aspen's winter sports enthusiasts, the dice were covered in P-Tex, a plastic material found on the bottoms of skis and snowboards. After the toss, the dice—visibly worse for the wear—were returned to the museum where they became part of Sone's exhibition.

Some of the nearly one thousand people who attended the dice toss, expressed disappointment that the large dice rolled only a third to a half of the way down the SuperPipe. But as Sone gave a command over a hand-held radio to the snowcat operators at the bottom of the pipe, to pick up the dice and toss them again—this time off of a large jump—the response came back negative. "We cannot get to the dice," they said, "the pipe is filled with kids!" And indeed it was. As the dice began to slow, scores of kids took the plunge sliding down the eighteen-foot-high walls of the SuperPipe to push the dice the rest of the way down. Simultaneously, they began to pull off the already shredding P-Tex, which they used as sleds to slide down the pipe again

Before 'Mt.66', 2006
Acrylic on paper/Acryl auf Papier
77.5 x 100.3 cm [30 $\frac{1}{2}$ x 39 $\frac{1}{2}$ in]

Dice, Storyboard, 2005
Acrylic on canvas / Acryl auf Leinwand
91.4 x 61 cm [36 x 24 in]

Snowy Mountain, 2005
Acrylic on masonite/Acryl auf Faserplatte
62.2 x 62.2 cm [24 1/2 x 24 1/2 in]

and again. In many ways, it was a massive free for all. In other ways, it was the quintessential cap to a fantastic project—an end so fitting that not even the artist himself could have imagined or choreographed it.

To commemorate *X-Art Show* and *Mt. 66*, Sone created a limited edition print featuring a two-dimensional rendering of the dice. The artist's color selection is idiosyncratic: hot pink, medium brown, conventional bright yellow, navy, and lime green. The print is designed so that it can be traditionally framed. The illustrations of the dice, however, feature tabs and cut lines so that they can also be cut out and folded to form miniature versions of the larger sculptures. Here again is another chance for the viewer to extend the range of, and become involved in, Sone's project.

For Sone, all aspects of art exhibition involve collaboration, and, to that end, Sone and favored partner Damon McCarthy compiled a film of all of the "collaborations" involved in the project, from skiing with museum staff and preliminary meetings with the Aspen Skiing Company to the building of the dice, the actual performance, and the celebratory after-party. The soundtrack of the resulting film features Sone's *Aspen Powder Cactus Band* performing improvisational music at the museum. The name of the band,

Ski Madonna # 1, 2005
Acrylic on canvas / Acryl auf Leinwand

Ski Madonna #2, 2005
Acrylic on canvas/Acryl auf Leinwand
91.4 x 61 cm [36 x 24 in]

Ski Madonna #3, 2006
Acrylic on canvas/Acryl auf Leinwand
61 x 45.7 cm [24 x 18 in]

Installation view / Installationsansicht Amusement Romana,
David Zwirner Gallery, 2004

Drawing for Snow Sculpture, 2000
Acrylic on canvas/Acryl auf Leinwand
53.3 x 65.4 cm [21 x 25 ³/⁴ in]

its members and the songs they play, were not fixed. The only unifying feature was that all the songs are about snow. Sone spent the day before the performance building cacti out of snow on the museum grounds with groups of children and their families. The notion of creating something inherently illogical—a desert plant in a winter landscape—is pure Sone. He finds pleasure in the everyday, transforming familiar people and things into something other. Alchemy is the essence of his practice.

In *Snowman* (2005), Sone painted a snowman equipped with a thought bubble. What do snowmen think about? According to Sone, they dream about warm, deserted islands filled with stereotypic palm trees and white sandy beaches! Many of the paintings in the *X-Art Show* form preparatory sketches for *Mt. 66*. *Dice, Storyboard* (2005) details how the dice would ideally travel down the mountain. Other works highlight ski behaviors, figures on chair lifts, skiing down mountains, and snowy mountain landscapes. The sport of skiing itself—little over a century old in America but dating back thousands of years in Scandinavia—has evolved over time. Sone himself is an excellent skier and was once a racer and tester of new skiing products. The mythology of sport and its inherent fusion with nature is celebrated within Sone's work.

It seems perfect that Japanese artist Yutaka Sone, who has been living in Los Angeles for the last six years, loves snow. Sone talks of the perfection and uniqueness of each single snowflake. Last winter, when Sone first visited Aspen, he was taken on a private tour of some of the best spots on Aspen Mountain: fresh powder, hidden trails, and shrines (the ski shrines of Aspen Mountain have been created by locals who have, for about two decades, been nailing pictures, license plates, silk flowers and other memorabilia to tree trunks in honor of their idols, heroes, and favorite celebrities). This day was memorialized in *Ski Madonna (#1)* (2005), a painting commissioned by the Aspen Art Museum in an innovative collaboration with the Aspen Skiing Company, to grace all 2005-2006 lift ticket products. In fact, skiers in Aspen could bring their lift tickets to the museum for fifty percent off admission. Sone's guide was Christy Sauer, Annual Fund Manager at the Aspen Art Museum and an experienced telemark skier. The artist's skis appear in the bottom center of the frame as he follows her through a quintessential Aspen alpine landscape. About the lift ticket, Sone has said, "I am happy people will be skiing with my *Ski Madonna* and I invite people to enjoy the many processes and to share new experiences through art." Sone's Madonna evokes a religious figure but without reference to a specific organized religion. Analogous to Mother Nature, she becomes abstracted but spiritual, revealing a knowing and a sense of truth.

Inspired by Marcel Duchamp and his *Nude Descending a Staircase* (1912), Sone subsequently painted *Ski Madonna (#2)* and *(#3)* both (2005). Sone described how Duchamp's work created a controversy when it was exhibited at the 1913 Armory Show in New York City. Duchamp and Sone share the desire to capture a female body in motion but diverge in the purity of representation in Sone's depiction. Sone intentionally created a eulogizing, "clean" image available for consumption and enjoyment by the family-oriented visitors to Aspen.

Fusing art with nature, sport, performance, and entertainment, Sone engages the audience with an idiosyncratically personal—and, curiously, almost universally relatable—illumination of the sublime in the everyday. Past projects include a film in

Dream, 2000
Acrylic on canvas / Acryl auf Leinwand
45 x 56 cm [17 3/4 x 22 in]

which the artist celebrates his birthday all day every day for more than a month, gorgeously detailed marble sculptures of Los Angeles freeway interchanges engulfed by hundreds of potted trees and sitting upon earthy odoriferous mulch, and human-scaled interactive sculptures. In one such project, Sone constructed a slide in the form of an infinity sign which viewers, in a Sisyphean effort, can continually walk up and slide down. The purpose of art, as Sone defines it, is to reveal "beautiful scenery that one never saw before." Sone's scenery is equally metaphorical and philosophical and thereby the quintessential match to Aspen's ideal of mind-body-spirit fusion.

X-Games Site Model #1, 2005
Wood, foam, acrylic paint / Holz, Acrylfarbe
61 x 106.7 x 43.2 cm [24 x 42 x 17 in]

Installation view/Installationsansicht *X-Art Show*
Aspen Art Museum, 2006

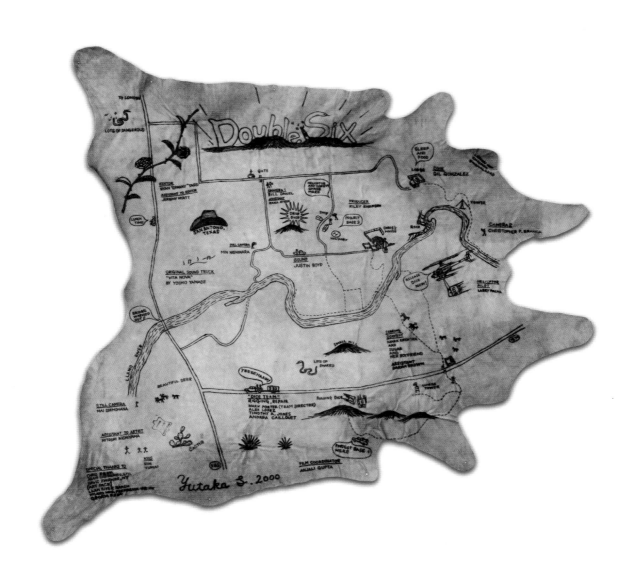

Double Six, 2000
Drawing burned onto cowhide with iron / Zeichnung auf
Rindsleder gebrannt, 233.6 x 259 cm [92 x 102 in]

Spiel und Spaß mit Yutaka Sone

Heidi Zuckerman Jacobson

Yutaka Sones Vorgehensweise ist skurril. Er malt und zeichnet, er macht Performances, Skulpturen und Installationen. Seine Ideen sprühen vor Leidenschaft und Inspiration. Er hat praktisch keinen Filter, nichts, was er zurückhält, ein Charakterzug, der ihn liebenswert macht und zwangsläufig zu Kooperationen führt. Er möchte, dass alle Teil des Prozesses werden, einschließlich des Sushi-Kochs, den er am Abend vor einem schweren Tag traf, an dem eine Skiwanderung an Aspens berüchtigtem Highland Bowl gefilmt werden sollte. Der Koch begleitete Sone, den Filmemacher Damon McCarthy, den Autor Benjamin Weissman, den Manager der Aspen Art Museum Facilities und Special Projects Patrick Storey, den Manager des Buttermilk Mountain Hans Hohl, sowie den Künstler Peter Doig, der gerade vor Ort an einem Projekt für das Aspen Art Museum arbeitete. Der Eklektizismus dieses Aufgebots des Künstlers ist typisch und absolut »X«.

Der Titel von Sones Ausstellung für das Aspen Art Museum, *X-Art Show*, bezieht sich auf die X-Games, ein Extremsport-Turnier, das jeden Winter am Buttermilk Mountain in Aspen stattfindet. Die Sportler sind berühmt für ihre aberwitzige Akrobatik auf Skiern, Snowboards, Motorrädern und Schneemobilen: Je größer die augenscheinliche Gefahr für die Teilnehmer desto intensiver ist der Nervenkitzel. Sone liebt alles, was »X« ist und damit verbunden die Auffassung, wonach der Kunst — insbesondere seiner eigenen — dieses Attribut zukommt. Die »X-ness« korrespondiert mit Sones Künstlertum ebenso wie mit seinem Stil: frisch, frei und extrem spannungsgeladen.

Im Rahmen seiner Arbeiten hat Sone bereits dreimal riesige Würfel konstruiert und war Zeuge ihres Einsatzes: in der Wüste außerhalb von San Antonio, Texas; bei der Eröffnung der Expo 2000 in Hannover; und von den Stufen des ikonischen Sydney Opera House in Australien. Sein lang gehegter Traum bestand darin, die Würfel von einem schneebedeckten Berg rollen zu sehen (Ein früheres Projekt in der Schweiz kam nie zur Ausführung).

Sones Würfel-Projekte implizieren Zufall, Mystizismus und die Transzendenz im Alltag. In Aspen wurde für eine Performance mit dem Titel *Mt. 66* ein Paar vom Künstler entworfener neu in Auftrag gegebener Würfel von rund 2,40 m Kantenlänge mit einem Tieflader durch die Stadt transportiert — vom Aspen Art Museum über die Main Street nach Buttermilk Mountain — und schließlich die x Games SuperPipe, eine wahrhaft gigantische Halfpipe, hinuntergeworfen. Inspiriert von Aspens Wintersport-Enthusiasten, wurden die Würfel mit P-Tex überzogen, einem Kunststoffmaterial, das für die Unterseite von Skiern und Snowboards verwendet wird. Nach dem Werfen wurden die Würfel — mit deutlich sichtbaren Gebrauchsspuren — zum Museum zurückgebracht und Teil von Sones Ausstellung.

Einige der nahezu tausend Menschen, die dem Würfelwurf beiwohnten, zeigten sich enttäuscht darüber, dass die großen Würfel nur etwa ein Drittel oder die Hälfte der SuperPipe hinabgerollt waren. Als Sone jedoch über Sprechfunk der Besatzung der Pistenraupe die Anweisung gab, die Würfel aufzuladen und nochmals zu werfen — dieses Mal von einer grossen Schanzen aus — erfolgte eine abschlägige Antwort: »Wir

Double Six (Performance at Artpace, San Antonio, Texas), 2000

können nicht an die Würfel heran, die Bahn ist voller Kinder!« Und genau so war es. Als die Würfel sich zu verlangsamen begannen, rutschten dutzende von Kindern und Jugendlichen die Sechs-Meter-Seitenwände der SuperPipe hinab, um die Würfel weiter hinunter zu schieben. Gleichzeitig begannen sie damit, das P-Tex abzureissen und es als Schlittenersatz zu benutzten, um wieder und wieder die Bahn hinabzurodeln. Einerseits herrschte in vielfacher Hinsicht ein großes Chaos. Andererseits ergab sich hierdurch der essenzielle Endpunkt eines fantastischen Projekts—ein Abschluss, der so stimmig war, dass selbst der Künstler ihn sich nicht hätte ausdenken oder choreografieren können.

Als Erinnerung an die *X-Art Show* und *Mt. 66* hat Sone einen Druck in limitierter Auflage geschaffen, eine zweidimensionale Wiedergabe der Würfel. Die Farbwahl des Künstlers ist eigenwillig: stechendes Pink, mittleres Braun, konventionelles leuchtendes Gelb, Marineblau und Limonengrün. Der Druck ist so ausgeführt, dass er auf traditionelle Weise gerahmt werden kann. Die Illustrationen der Würfel haben jedoch Falz- und Schnittlinien, so dass sie auch als Bastelvorlage für Miniaturversionen der großen Skulpturen verwendet werden können. Es handelt sich abermals um eine Möglichkeit, die Reichweite von Sones Projekt zu vergrößern und an ihm teilzuhaben.

Würfelwurf / Throwing the Dice
(Performance at Expo 2000, Hannover), 2000

Dice, X-Games, 2005
Acrylic on canvas / Acryl auf Leinwand
76.2 x 62.2 cm [30 x 24 ¹/² in]

Für Sone beinhaltet jeder Aspekt einer Kunstausstellung Kooperation. Zu diesem Zweck haben Sone und sein Lieblingspartner Damon McCarthy einen Film gedreht über sämtliche »Kooperationen«, die Teil des Projektes sind: vom Skifahren mit Mitarbeitern des Museums und vorbereitenden Treffen mit der Aspen Skiing Company bis hin zur Herstellung der Würfel, der eigentlichen Performance, und der anschließenden Party. Der Soundtrack des so entstandenen Films stammt von Sones *Aspen Powder Cactus Band* aus einem Auftritt mit improvisierter Musik im Museum. Der Name der Band, ihre Mitglieder und ihr Repertoire waren keineswegs festgelegt. Das einzig gemeinsame Merkmal bestand darin, dass alle Lieder von Schnee handelten. Sone verbrachte den Tag vor der Performance mit Kindern und ihren Familien beim Bauen von Kakteen aus Schnee. Die Idee der Erschaffung von etwas wesentlich Unlogischem—eine Wüstenpflanze in einer Winterlandschaft—ist Sone pur. Er findet Vergnügen im Alltäglichen, verwandelt gewöhnliche Dinge und Menschen in etwas Anderes. Das Wesen seiner Arbeit ist Alchemie.

In *Snowman* (2005) hat Sone einen Schneemann mit einer Denkblase gemalt. Was denken Schneemänner? Sone zufolge träumen sie von warmen einsamen Inseln voll stereotyper Palmen und weißen Sandstränden! Viele der Bilder in der *X-Art Show* bilden Vorarbeiten zu *Mt. 66*. *Dice, Storyboard* (2005) zeichnet detailliert vor, wie die Würfel idealerweise den Berg herunterrollen. Andere Arbeiten widmen sich dem Verhalten von Skiern, Figuren auf Sesselliften, der Abfahrt vom Berg auf Skiern und verschneiten Berglandschaften. Der Skisport—in den USA nur wenig älter als hundert Jahre, seit Jahrtausenden jedoch in Skandinavien betrieben—hat eine Evolution durchlaufen. Sone selbst ist ein exzellenter Skifahrer und war einmal Rennfahrer und Testfahrer für neue Skiausrüstungen. Die Mythologie des Sports und seine inhärente Verschmelzung mit der Natur werden in Sones Arbeiten gefeiert.

Es erscheint geradezu perfekt, dass der japanische Künstler Yutaka Sone, der seit sechs Jahren in Los Angeles lebt, Schnee liebt. Sone spricht von der Perfektion und Einzigartigkeit jeder einzelnen Schneeflocke. Im vergangenen Winter, als Sone Aspen erstmals besuchte, bekam er eine Privatführung zu einigen der besten Flecken in den Bergen um Aspen: frischer Pulverschnee, versteckte Pfade und sogenannte Schreine (Die Ski-Schreine von Aspen Mountain sind von Ortsansässigen angelegt worden, die seit ungefähr zwanzig Jahren Fotos, Autokennzeichen, Seidenblumen und andere Memorabilien zu Ehren ihrer Idole, Helden, und Lieblinge an Baumstämme nageln). Jenem Tag wurde mit *Ski Madonna (#1)* (2005) ein Denkmal gesetzt, einem Gemälde im Auftrag des Aspen Art Museum in einer innovativen Zusammenarbeit mit der Aspen Skiing Company, welches sämtliche Lift-Tickets des Winters 2005/2006 ziert. Tatsächlich konnten Skifahrer in Aspen zum Tausch für ihre Lift-Tickets das Museum zum halben Preis besuchen. Sones Führerin auf jenem Ausflug war Christy Sauer, Annual Fund Manager am Aspen Art Museum und eine erfahrene Skilangläuferin. Die Skier des Künstlers erscheinen in der Mitte des unteren Bildrands, während er ihr durch eine Berglandschaft folgt, die charakteristisch für Aspen ist. Zum Lift-Ticket sagt Sone: »Ich bin froh, dass die Menschen mit meiner *Ski Madonna* fahren werden, und ich lade die Menschen ein, die vielen Abläufe zu genießen und an neuen Erfahrungen teilzuhaben, die durch Kunst entstehen.« Sones Madonna evoziert eine Gestalt aus dem Bereich der Religion, ohne aber auf eine bestimmte organisierte Religion zu verweisen. Analog zu Mutter Natur wird sie abstrahiert auf ihre Spiritualität und bekundet eine Weisheit und einen Sinn für Wahrheit.

Mt. 66 (Performance at Buttermilk Mountain, Aspen), 2006

In Anklang an Marcel Duchamp und seinen *Akt, eine Treppe hinabsteigend* (1912) hat Sone später *Ski Madonna (#2)* und *(#3)*, (beide 2005) gemalt. Sone beschrieb, wie Duchamps Werk eine Kontroverse hervorrief, als es 1913 auf der Armory Show in New York ausgestellt wurde. Duchamp und Sone haben gemeinsam, den weiblichen Körper in der Bewegung festhalten zu wollen, unterscheiden sich aber in der Reinheit der Repräsentation in Sones Abbildung. Sone schafft mit Absicht ein elogisches, »sauberes« Bild, das zum Verbrauch und Vergnügen für die familienbewussten Besucher Aspens bestimmt ist.

Mit der Fusion von Kunst, Natur, Sport, Performance und Unterhaltung setzt Sone das Publikum seiner eigenwilligen persönlichen — und, überraschenderweise, beinahe universell anwendbaren — Illumination des Sublimen im Alltäglichen aus. Unter seinen früheren Projekten finden sich ein Film, in dem der Künstler über einen Monat hinweg jeden Tag den ganzen Tag lang seinen Geburtstag feiert, wunderbar detaillierte Marmorskulpturen von Autobahnkreuzen in Los Angeles, die von hunderten von in Kübeln gepflanzten Bäumen gesäumt werden und die auf einem erdigen, duftenden Mulch liegen sowie lebensgroße interaktive Skulpturen. In einem dieser Projekte konstruiert Sone eine Rutsche in der Form des Unendlichkeitssymbols, welche die Betrachter in einer Sisyphos-gleichen Anstrengung immer neu besteigen und wieder hinabrutschen können. Das Ziel der Kunst bestehe darin, so definiert Sone, eine »schöne Landschaft zu enthüllen, die noch nie zuvor gesehen wurde.« Sones Landschaft ist zugleich metaphorisch und philosophisch und erfüllt dadurch wesentlich Aspens Ideal einer Fusion aus Bewusstsein, Körper und Geist.

Giant Snow Leopard, 2004-2005
Marble/Marmor
63.5 x 228.6 x 185.4 [25 x 90 x 73 in]

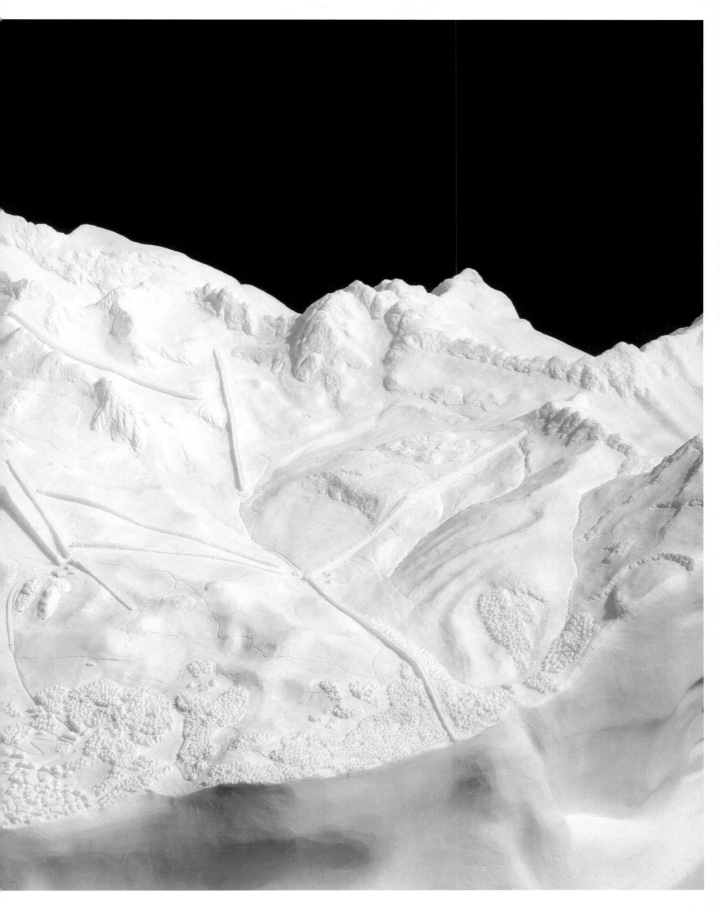

Preparatory drawing for / Entwurf für *Like Looking for Snow Leopard*
Kunsthalle Bern, 2006

Biography/Biographie

Yutaka Sone

Born/Geboren 1965, Shizuoka, Japan.
Lives/Lebt in Los Angeles, California.

EDUCATION/AUSBILDUNG
1992 M.A. in Architecture, Tokyo Geijutsu
     University
1988 B.F.A., Tokyo Geijutsu University

SOLO EXHIBITIONS / EINZELAUSSTELLUNGEN

2006 Like Looking for Snow Leopard, Kunsthalle
Bern, Bern, Switzerland
X-Art Show, Aspen Museum of Art, Aspen, CO
Forecast: Snow, The Renaissance Society at
The University of Chicago, Chicago, IL

2005 Snow, Gallery Side 2, Tokyo, Japan

2004 Amusement Romana, David Zwirner,
New York, NY
Vertical Travel, Bowie Van Valen,
Amsterdam, The Netherlands
Amusement Romana, Gallery Side 2, Tokyo,
Japan

2003 Yutaka Sone: Jungle Island, MOCA at the
Geffen Contemporary, Los Angeles, CA
Japanese Pavilion, La Bienale di Venezia,
Venice, Italy
White Cave, Akiyoshidai International Art
Village, Mine-gun, Japan

2002 Travel to Double River Island, Toyota
Municipal Museum of Art, Toyota City, Japan

2000 Double Six, Artpace, San Antonio, TX

1999 David Zwirner, New York, NY
Kohji Ogura Gallery, Nagoya, Japan
Alpine Attack, Sogetsu Art Museum, Tokyo,
Japan

1998 Magic Stick / Happy Birthday, AARA,
Bangkok, Thailand
At the End of All the Journeys, Shiseido Art
House, Kakegawa, Japan
At the End of All the Journeys, Navin Taxi
Gallery, Bangkok, Thailand

1997 Amusement, Gallery Side 2, Tokyo, Japan
At the End of All the Journeys, Hiroshima
City Contemporary Art Museum, Hiroshima,
Japan

1996 Future Perfect, Bunkamura Gallery, Tokyo,
Japan
Scoop, Mitaka City Arts Foundation, Tokyo,
Japan

1995 Departures, Roentgen Kunst Institute,
Tokyo, Japan

1994 Space Luxury Art, Hosomi Gallery, Tokyo,
Japan
Her 19th Foot, NICAF, Yokohama, Japan
Mars Gallery, Tokyo, Japan

1993 One hand clapping, Yokohama Galleria,
Yokohama, Japan
Her 19th foot, Contemporary Art Center,
Art Tower Mito, Mito, Japan

GROUP EXHIBITIONS / GRUPPENAUSSTELLUNGEN

2005 Untitled Folly, Bowie Van Valen, Amsterdam,
The Netherlands
EindhovenIstanbul, Van Abbemuseum,
Eindhoven, The Netherlands
Bidibidobidiboo, Works form the Sandretto
Re Rebaudengo Collection, Fondazione
Sandretto Re Rebaudengo, Turin, Italy
Chikaku, Time and Memory in Japan,
Kunsthaus Graz / Camera Austria, Graz,
Austria
Monuments for the USA, CCA Wattis
Institute for Contemporary Arts, San
Francisco, CA
IDYL – As to Answer that Picture, Middel-
heim Open Air Museum, Antwerp, Belgium,
curated by / kuratiert von Philippe Pirotte
Desenhos: A-Z [Drawings: A-Z], Porta 33,
Ilha da Madeira, Portugal
Surface, Lucas Schoormans Gallery,
New York, NY
Universal Experience: Art, Life & the
Tourists Eye, MCA Chicago, Chicago, IL
25: Twenty-five Years of the Deutsche Bank
Collection, Deutsche Guggenheim, Berlin,
Germany

2004 Whitney Biennial 2004, Whitney Museum of
Contemporary Art, New York, NY
100 Artists See God, Independent Curators
International, New York, NY [itinerary /
Wanderausstellung: The Jewish Museum,
San Francisco, CA; Laguna Art Museum,
Laguna Beach, CA; Contemporary Art
Center of Virginia, Virginia Beach, VA;
Albright College Freedman Art Gallery,
Reading, PA]
Brainstorming: Topographie de la morale,
Centre National d'art et du Paysage de
Vassivière, île de Vassivière, France
CLIMATS, cyclothymie des paysages,
Centre nationale d'art et du paysage,
Vassivière, France

2003 Metascape, The Cleveland Museum of Art,
Cleveland, OH
The Gift. Generous offering, insidious
hospitality, Block Museum of Art at
Northwestern University, Chicago, IL
The Sharjah International Arts Biennial,
Sharjah, United Arab Emirates
The Summer of 2003, Galerie Paul
Andriesse, Amsterdam, The Netherlands
Happy Trail, Shiseido Gallery, Tokyo, Japan

2002 Gegen und sich hingeben. Klagenfurt
Stadtgalerie, Klagenfurt, Austria
The Gift. Generous offering, insidious
hospitality, Scottsdale Museum of
Contemporary Art, Scottsdale, AZ

Loop, P.S. 1 Contemporary Art Center, Long Island City, NY
25th Biennal de São Paulo, São Paulo, Brazil
The House of Fiction, Sammlung Hauser und Wirth in der Lokremise St. Gallen, St. Gallen, Switzerland
13th Biennale of Sydney, Sydney, Australia
Das Geschenk, Stadt Galerie Klagenfurt, Germany
Expect: Art, The What to Expect Foundation, New York, NY
The Gift. Generous offering, insidious hospitality, Bronx Museum, Bronx, NY
(The World May Be) Fantastic, Biennale of Sydney, Sydney, Australia

2001 New Works: 00.4, Artpace, A Foundation for Contemporary Art, San Antonio, TX
Public Offerings, The Museum of Contemporary Art, Los Angeles, CA
The Gift. Generous offering, insidious hospitality, Palazzo delle Papesse, Centro Arte Contemporanea, Siena, Italy
24 Gardens – one day/Garden Landscape Ostwestfalen-Lippe 2001, Gutspark Böckel, Germany
Phillip Morris Art Award, Tokyo and Osaka, Japan
Techno Landscape, toward newer texture of the world, ICC Gallery, Tokyo, Japan
About the Bayberry Bush, The Parrish Art Museum, Southampton, NY
Yokohama 2001: International Triennale of Contemporary Art, Yokohama, Japan
7th International Istanbul Biennial 2001, Istanbul, Turkey
Loop, Kunsthalle der Hypo Kulturstiftung, Munich, Germany
I ♥ NY, David Zwirner, New York, NY

2000 Acquisizione recenti/Recent Acquisitions, Fondazione Sandretto Re Rebaudengo per l'Arte, Palazzo Re Rebaudengo, Guarene d'Alba, Italy
From a Distance: Landscape in Contemporary Art, The Institute of Contemporary Art, Boston, MA
In Between. The Art Project of Expo 2000, Expo 2000, Hannover, Germany
Le Jardin, Académie de France à Rome-Villa Medici, Rome, Italy
The Greenhouse Effect, Serpentine Gallery, London, UK
Time, Bergen Kunstmuseum, Bergen, Norway
Déjà Vu, Center for Curatorial Studies, Bard College, Annandale-on-Hudson, NY

1999 Cities on the Move 7, Kiasma, Helsinki, Finland
Fancy Dance – Contemporary Japanese Art After 1990, Artsonje Center, Seoul, Korea [itinerary/Wanderausstellung: Artsonje Museum, Kyongiu, Korea]
Cities on the Move 5, Hayward Gallery, London, UK
New Life: 11 Artists from Denmark and Sweden in Tokyo, Contemporary Art Factory, Tokyo, Japan
Cities on the Move 4, Louisiana Museum, Humblebaek, Denmark
Unfinished History, Museum of Contemporary Art, Chicago, IL

1998 Unfinished History, Walker Art Center, Minneapolis, MN
Cities on the Move 3, PS1 Contemporary Art Center, Queens, NY
Cities on the Move 2, CAPC, Musée d'art Moderne, Bordeaux, France
SHOOT AT THE CHAOS-Age of the Electronic Image, Spiral/Wacoal Art Center, Tokyo, Japan

1997 Cities on the Move 1, Wiener Secession, Vienna, Austria
Skulpturen Projekte, Munster, Germany
Du Construit, Du Paysage, Centre Regional d'art Contemporain, Sete, France
Promenade in Asia, Shiseido Gallery, Tokyo, Japan; curated by/kuratiert von Shimizu Toshio
VOCA, Ueno-no-mori Museum, Tokyo, Japan

1996 Art Scene 1990-1996, Contemporary Art Center, Art Tower Mito, Mito, Japan
Interzones, Kunstforeningen, Copenhagen, Denmark
Join Me! One Night Artist's Cafe, Spiral Wacoal Art Center, Tokyo, Japan
Video Art on the Edge, Kita Kanto Museum of Fine Arts, Maebashi, Japan

1995 Chiang Mai Social Installation, Chiang Mai, Thailand
Ripple Across The Water, The Watari Museum of Contemporary Art, Watari-um, Tokyo; curated by/kuratiert von Jan Hoet
Nutopi, Rooseum, Malmo, Sweden; curated by/kuratiert von Lars Nittve
Visions of Happiness, The Japan Foundation ASIAN Culture Center, Tokyo, Japan

1994 Shinjuku Shonen Art, Shinjuku, Tokyo, Japan

Himalaya 1986, 2005
Acrylic on canvas / Acryl auf Leinwand
45.7 x 61 cm [18 x 24 in]

Bibliography/Bibliographie

Yutaka Sone

2006

Stabler, Ben. "Snow Job" Chicago Reader (February 17, 2006), Section One pp. 28-29, [ill.].

AK. "Current Issue" artkrush (February 22, 2006), Issue #26, [ill.].

Ng, Elaine. "Yutaka Sone: The Blizzard of 2006." Asia Art Pacific, (Spring 2006), pp. 70-74.

2005

"On the Ground." Artforum International, (December 2005), pp. 218-219.

2004

Diez, Renato. "Alla Biennale del Whitney: Torna la Pittura." Arte, (April 2004), pp. 104-111.

Montreuil, Gregory. "Yutaka Sone." Contemporary Magazine, Issue 64 (2004), pp. 98-101.

Reckitt, Helena. "Frieze Art Fair." Art AsiaPacific, No. 29 (Winter 2004), p. 23.

Saltz, Jerry. "The OK Corral." The Village Voice, Voice Choices (March 17-23, 2004), p. C80.

Wolf, Matt. "Yutaka Sone." Flash Art, Vol. XXXVII, No. 236 (May – June 2004), p. 83.

"Yutaka Sone." The New Yorker, (March 29, 2004), p. 17.

2003

Itoi, Kay. "Land of the rising stars." The Art Newspaper, (2003). www.theartnewspaper.com/news/article.asp?idart=11338

Knight, Christopher. "An RIP for the freeways." Los Angeles Times Calendar Weekend, (May 8, 2003), pp. E4-E5.

Reiko, Yuyama. "Yutaka Sone: Sit Up Late." Switch, Vol. 21, No. 10 (October 2003), pp. 178-179.

Roug, Louise. "In L.A. for art's sake." Los Angeles Times Calendar Sunday. (May 4, 2003), pp. E72-E73.

Sone, Yutaka. "Guns and Roses." V Magazine, No. 25 (Sept/Oct 2003).

"La Biennale di Venezia." Bijutsu Techo, Vol. 55, No. 838 (2003), pp. 12-17.

2002

Hirayoshi, Yukihiro. "Travel to Double River Island." Bijutsu Techo, Vol. 54, No. 825 (September 2002), pp. 109-115.

"Art." Studio Voice, Vol. 321 (September 2002), p. 88.

2001

Philip Morris Art Award: 24 Winners from 1996-2000, New York. (2001), pp. 58-59.

Hug. Catherine. "Egofugal/Egokac: Fugue from Ego for the Next Emergence." Tema Celeste. (November-December 2001), pp. 98-99.

Goddard, Dan R. "Japanese artist has a high-roller going at ArtPace" San Antonio Express-News (January 2, 2001), p. 4D.

2000

Nishizawa, Miki. "Artist steps up plans for alpine attack" The Japan Times (February 14, 2000), p. 14.

Oliver, Retha. "Ten-gallon installation" San Antonio Current (December 28, 2000 – January 3, 2001), p. 14.

O'Grady, Janet. "New Meets Old" Aspen Magazine (Holiday 2000/01), pp. 134-143.

1999

Cotter, Holland. "Yutaka Sone." The New York Times. (September 24, 1999), p. E36.

Grabner, Michelle. "Unfinished History." Frieze. (May 1999), p. 95.

Montreuil, Gregory. "Yutaka Sone." New Art Examiner. (December/January 1999/2000), p. 54.

Saltz, Jerry. "Where the Boys Are." Village Voice. (October 5, 1999), p. 187.

Yablonsky, Linda. "Yutaka Sone." Time Out NY. (September 23, 1999), p. 63.

Asahi Shimbun Weekly (February 15, 1999).

Yomiuri Newspaper (February 6, 1999).

1998

Review TOKIO (January 1998), p. 203.

Shizuoka Newspaper (January 3, 1998), p. 39.

Nishihara, Min. "Tokyo by Night." Siksi. (Summer 1998), pp. 48-51.

1997

Araki, Natumi. "Amusement." Bijutu Techo. (January 1997), pp. 202-203.

Inoue, Shoji. "An artist who brings us to an unknown moment." Tokyo Shinbun. (September 6, 1997), pp. 202-203.

Kawai, Sumie. "Contemporary Art festival." Bijutsu Techo. (September, 1997), p. 48.

Nishihara, Min. "Muenster, Open Door." Studio Voice. (September, 1997), p. 124.

Onishi, Wakoudo. "Art in Europe '97." Asahi Shinbun. (August 16, 1997)

"Muenster Sculpture Projekt, Yutaka Sone", Kunstforum, pp. 344-345.

"New Landscape, New Emotion" (interview), Bijutsu Techo, (April, 1997), pp. 113-125.

Asaki Newspaper (August 7, 1997)

Tokyo Newspaper (September 6, 1997)

1996

Bellars, Peter. "Mission Impossible." Asahi Evening News. (June 23, 1996), p. 7.

Inagaki, Naoko. Nikkei Shinbun. (December 22, 1996), p. 19.

Kurosawa, Shin. "Yutaka Sone-Scoop." Studio Voice. (June, 1996), p. 75.

Nikkei Newspaper (December 22, 1996), p. 19.

1995

Holmberg, Diana. "Lekfull balankonst." HD Allmant, (June 3, 1995), p. 3.
Nishihara, Min. "Rat Race." Studio Voice. (April, 1995), p. 87.
Lind, Maria. "Nutopi." Frieze. (September, 1995), p. 73.
Matsui, Midori. "Departures." Studio Voice. (November, 1995), p. 73.

1993

Studio Voice (August 1993)

CATALOGUES / KATALOGE

2005

Eindhoven, The Netherlands. Van Abbemuseum. EindhovenIstanbul, 2005. Texts by / Texte von Kerryn Greenberg and/und Eva Meyer-Hermann.
Cologne, Germany. Kunsthaus Graz. Chikaku: Time and Memory in Japan, 2005. Texts by / Texte von Christine Frisinghelli, Peter Pakesch et al.
Frankfurt am Main, Germany. Deutsche Bank Art. 25. Twenty-five Years of the Deutsche Bank Collection, 2005. Texts by / Texte von Ariane Grigoteit et al.
Graz, Austria. Kunsthaus Graz / Camera Austria. Chikaku. Time and Memory in Japan, 2005. Texts by / Texte von Ryuta Imafuku, Toshiharu Ito, Makato Sei Watanabe, Krystyna Wilkoszewska, and/und Yoko Tawada.
San Antonio, TX. Artpace. Artists Salute Artpace, auction catalogue, 2005.

2004

New York, NY. Independent Curators International. 100 Artists See God, 2004. Texts by / Texte von John Baldessari, Meg Cranston, Thomas McEvilley.
New York, NY. The Whitney Museum of American Art. Whitney Biennial 2004, 2004. Texts by / Texte von Chrissie Iles, Shamim Momin, Debra Singer et al.

2003

Tokyo, Japan. Shiseido Culture Design Department. Happy Trail I: The Document, 2003. Text by / Text von Benjamin Weissman.
Tokyo, Japan. Shiseido Culture Design Department. Happy Trail II: The Installation, 2003. Text by / Text von Haruko Kohno.

2002

Istanbul, Turkey. Ecofugal: 7th International Istanbul Biennial, 2002. Text by / Text von Yuko Hasegawa.
Koln, Germany. Taschen. Art Now, 2002. Edited by / Herausgegeben von Burkhard Riemschneider, and/und Uta Grosenick.
New York, New York. The What to Expect Foundation. Expect: Art, 2002.

São Paulo. Brazil. Fundação Bienal de São Paulo. Paises 25th Bienal de São Paulo: The 12th City, 2002.
Sydney, Australia. Biennale of Sydney, Ltd. (The World May Be) Fantastic – 13th Biennale of Sydney, 2002. Edited by / Herausgegeben von Ewen McDonald.
Toyota City, Japan. Toyota Municipal Museum of Art. Travel to Double River Island, 2002.

2001

Los Angeles, CA. Museum of Contemporary Art. Public Offerings, 2001. Edited by / Herausgegeben von Howard Singerman.
Munich, Germany. Kunsthalle des Hypo-Kultur-stiftung. Loop-Alles auf Anfang. Edited by / Herausgegeben von Anselm Franke and/und Maika Pollack.
Southampton, NY. The Parrish Art Museum. About the Bayberry Bush, 2001. Edited by / Herausgegeben von Ingrid Schaffner and/und Melissa Feldman.
Istanbul, Turkey. Ecofugal: 7th International Istanbul Biennial, 2001. Text by / Text von Yuko Hasegawa.

2000

Hanover, Germany. EXPO 2000. In Between. The Art Project of Expo 2000, 2000. Edited by / Herausgegeben von Wilfried Dickhoff and/und Kasper König.
Rome, Italy. Académie de France à Rome. Villa Medicis. La Ville / Le Jardin / La Mémoire, Texts by / Texte von Hans-Ulrich Obrist.
London, England. The Serpentine Gallery. The Greenhouse Effect, 2000. Texts by / Texte von Susan Morley, Ralph Rugoff and/und Lisa Corrin.

1999

Artsonje Museum and/und Artsonje Center. Fancy Dance – Contemporary Japanese Art After 1990, 1999. Text by / Text von Yuko Hasegawa.
Académie de France à Rome-Villa Medicis, La Memoire-99, 1999.
Helsinki, Finland. Museum of Contemporary Art, Cities on the Move 7, 1999.
Humblebaek, Denmark. Louisiana Museum, Cities on the Move 4, 1999.
Tokyo, Japan. Sogetsu Art Museum. Alpine Attack, 1999. Edited by / Herausgegeben von Hiromi Ohashi.
Torino, Italy. Fondazione Sandretto Re Rebaudengo per L'Arte. Dreams. 1999.

1998

Minneapolis, Minnesota. Walker Art Center. Unfinished History, 1998. Edited by / Heraus-gegeben von Kathleen McLean and/und Pamela Johnson.

1997

Bordeaux, France. Musée d'art contemporain de
Bordeaux. Cities on the Move. 1997. Edited by/
Herausgegeben von Hou Hanru and/und
Hans-Ulrich Obrist.

Münster, Germany. Verlag Gerd Hatje. Sculpture.
Projects in Münster 1997, 1997. Edited by/
Herausgegeben von Klaus Bußmann, Kasper
König, Florian Matzner.

Münster, Germany. Verlag Gerd Hatje. Unbuilt
Roads – 107 Unrealized Projects, 1997. Edited
by/Herausgegeben von Hans-Ulrich Obrist.

Tokyo, Japan. Shiseido Corporate Culture
Department. Promenade in Asia, 1997. Edited
by/Herausgegeben von Irie Yoshiyuki and/und
Higuchi Masaki.

1996

Tokyo. Japan. Mitaka City Arts Foundation.
Building Romance, 1996. Text by/Text von Min
Nishihara.

1995

Copenhagen, Denmark. Kunstforeinengen.
Interzones, 1995. Text by/Text von Octavio
Zaya.

Malmö, Sweden. Rooseum. Nutopi, 1995. Text by
/Text von Lars Nittve and/und Shin Kurosawa.

1994

Tokyo. Japan. Yokohama Galleria. The man who
digs a bottomless swamp-or, an absurd Duchamp,
1994. Text by/Text von Yuko Hasegawa.

1993

Mito, Japan. Art Tower Mito. Desire,
Impossibility and the Other Being, 1993.
Text by/Text von Shin Kurosawa.

MISCELLANEOUS/VERSCHIEDENES

2004

Film Screening, Pompidou Center, Paris, France.

Biographies Curators and Authors/ Biografien KuratorInnen und AutorInnen

Benjamin Weissman

Benjamin Weissman is the author of two books of
short fiction, most recently *Headless*.
His writing about art and skiing have appeared
recently in *Frieze*, *Modern Painters*, and *Powder*.
He teaches at Art Center College of Design,
Pasadena, and Otis College of Art, Los Angeles.

Benjamin Weissman ist der Autor zweier Bände
mit Kurzgeschichten, von denen der jüngste den
Titel *Headless* trägt. Seine Artikel über Kunst
und Skilaufen sind rezent in *Frieze*, *Modern
Painters* und *Powder* erschienen. Er unterrichtet
am Art Center College of Design, Pasadena, und
dem Otis College of Art, Los Angeles.

Philippe Pirotte

Since 2005 Philippe Pirotte (Antwerp, 1972) is
the Director and Chief Curator of the Kunsthalle
Bern in Switzerland, where he organised solo-
projects with Anne-Mie van Kerckhoven, Corey
McCorkle, Knut Åsdam and Carla Arocha as well
as group exhibitions with Stefan Brüggeman,
Pavel Büchler, Gaylen Gerber, Stephen Prina,
Ivan Grubanov, Suchan Kinoshita, Pamela
Rosenkranz, Gert Verhoeven, Mike Bouchet,
Tommy Simoens, Gardar Eide Einarsson,
Roberto Cuoghi and others.
Also in 2005 he realized the group exhibition
IDYL – As to answer that picture for the Middel-
heim Open Air Museum in Antwerp including
Miroslaw Balka, Lee Bul, Yutaka Sone, Mark
Lewis, and others.
He is founding director of objectif_exhibitions in
Antwerp and since 2002 he is senior advisor at the
Rijksakademie in Amsterdam, the Netherlands. He
published essays and texts on contemporary art in
various books, catalogues and magazines, including
texts on Luc Tuymans, Pascale Marthine Tayou,
Yun Fei-Ji, Kris Fierens, Corey McCorkle, Carla
Arocha and Ivan Grubanov.

Seit 2005 ist Philippe Pirotte (geb. 1972 in
Antwerpen) der Direktor und leitende Kurator
der Kunsthalle Bern, wo er Einzelausstellungen
organisierte mit Anne-Mie van Kerckhoven,
Corey McCorkle, Knut Åsdam und Carla Arocha
sowie Gruppenausstellungen mit u.a. Stefan
Brüggeman, Pavel Büchler, Gaylen Gerber,
Stephen Prina, Ivan Grubanov, Suchan Kinoshita,

Pamela Rosenkranz, Gert Verhoeven, Mike Bouchet, Tommy Simoens, Gardar Eide Einarsson, Roberto Cuoghi.

Ebenfalls im Jahr 2005 realisierte er die Gruppen-ausstellung *IDYL – As to answer that picture* im Middelheim Skulpturenpark in Antwerpen mit unter anderen Miroslaw Balka, Lee Bul, Yutaka Sone und Mark Lewis.

Er ist der Gründungsdirektor von objectif_exhibitions in Antwerpen und seit 2002 ist er Berater an der Rijksakademie in Amsterdam. Er hat Essays und Beiträge zur zeitgenössischen Kunst in einer Reihe von Büchern, Katalogen und Zeitschriften veröffentlicht, u.a. Texte zu Luc Tuymans, Pascale Marthine Tayou, Yun Fei-Ji, Kris Fierens, Corey McCorkle, Carla Arocha und Ivan Grubanov.

Hamza Walker

Hamza Walker, Associate Curator and Director of Education at The Renaissance Society, is a recipient of the 2004 Walter Hopps Award for Curatorial Achievement and 1999 Curators Grant from the Peter Norton Family Foundation. He was educated at the University of Chicago (BA, Art History) and studied at the School of the Art Institute of Chicago. He is also an adjunct faculty member at the School of the Art Institute of Chicago, a freelance curator, and frequent contributor to art publications including *Artforum* and *Parkett*.

Hamza Walker, Kurator und Leiter Kunstvermittlung an der Renaissance Society, erhielt 2004 den Walter Hopps Award for Curatorial Achievement (Preis für Kuratorische Leistungen) und 1999 das Kuratorenstipendium der Peter Norton Family Foundation. Er studierte an der University of Chicago (BA in Kunstgeschichte) sowie an der School of the Art Institute of Chicago. Er ist ebenfalls assoziiertes Fakultätsmitglied an der School of the Art Institute of Chicago, selbstständiger Kurator und schreibt regelmäßig Beiträge für Kunstzeitschriften wie *Artforum* und *Parkett*.

Heidi Zuckerman Jacobson

Heidi Zuckerman Jacobson is the Director and Chief Curator of the Aspen Art Museum, appointed in 2005. Her Aspen Art Museum projects include one-person exhibitions with Simon Evans, Yutaka Sone, Javier Téllez, Doug Aitken, and Pedro Reyes. From 1999-2005 she was the Phyllis Wattis MATRIX Curator at the University of California, Berkeley Art Museum and Pacific Film Archive, where she curated more than forty solo exhibitions of international contemporary artists such as Peter Doig, Tobias Rehberger, Shirin Neshat, Teresita Fernández, Julie Mehretu, Doug Aitken, Tacita Dean, Wolfgang Laib, Ernesto Neto, Simryn Gill, Jun Nguyen-Hatsushiba, Sanford Biggers, and T.J. Wilcox. She also produced a digital videodisc documenting the 1999-2000 MATRIX season in which the artists are represented by visual walkthroughs of their exhibitions, as well as excerpts from their artist's talks and interviews with MATRIX Curator Heidi Zuckerman Jacobson. Formerly she was the Assistant Curator of 20th-century Art at The Jewish Museum, New York. Ms. Zuckerman Jacobson has lectured extensively on contemporary art, independently curated exhibitions internationally, and served in numerous advisory capacities. She received her BA from the University of Pennsylvania and her MA from CUNY/Hunter College, New York where she wrote her thesis on video art. She is a graduate of Christie's Education and received a diploma from the Royal Society of Art, London. Ms. Zuckerman Jacobson has taught at UC Berkeley, CUNY/Hunter College, and is on the faculty of the California College of the Arts as a professor in the Masters of Curatorial Studies program.

Heidi Zuckerman Jacobson ist seit 2005 Direktorin und leitende Kuratorin des Aspen Art Museum. Unter ihren Projekten für das Aspen Art Museum sind Einzelausstellungen von Simon Evans, Yutaka Sone, Javier Téllez, Doug Aitken, und Pedro Reyes. Von 1999 bis 2005 war sie Phyllis Wattis MATRIX Kuratorin an der University of California, Berkeley Art Museum und Pacific Film Archive. Dort kuratierte sie mehr als vierzig Einzelausstellungen von zeitgenössischen internationalen Künstlern wie Peter Doig, Tobias Rehberger, Shirin Neshat, Teresita Fernández, Julie Mehretu, Doug Aitken, Tacita Dean, Wolfgang Laib, Ernesto Neto, Simryn Gill, Jun Nguyen-Hatsushiba, Sanford Biggers und T.J. Wilcox. Sie hat ebenfalls ein digitales Video produziert, das die 1999-2000 MATRIX Saison dokumentiert und in dem die Künstler anhand von virtuellen Ausstellungsdurchgängen sowie Ausschnitten aus Künstlergesprächen und Interviews mit der MATRIX Kuratorin Heidi Zuckerman Jacobson präsentiert werden. Zuvor war sie Assistenzkuratorin für Kunst des 20. Jahrhunderts am Jewish Museum, New York. Frau Zuckerman Jacobson hat eine Vielzahl von Vorträgen über zeitgenössische Kunst gehalten, als selbstständige Kuratorin internationale Ausstellungen kuratiert und ist in zahlreichen beratenden Funktionen tätig gewesen. Sie erlangte den akademischen Grad eines BA an der University of Pennsylvania und den eines MA am CUNY/ Hunter College, New York, wo sie eine Magisterarbeit über Videokunst schrieb. Sie hat eine Ausbildung bei Christie's Education abgeschlossen und erhielt ein Diplom von der Royal Society of Art, London. Frau Zuckerman Jacobson hat an der UC Berkeley und dem CUNY/Hunter College unterrichtet und gehört der Fakultät der California College of the Arts an als Professor im Programm zum Erwerb des Grades eines Master of Curatorial Studies.

Susanne Ghez

Susanne Ghez was educated at Bryant College and studied art history at the University of California, Berkeley, and Columbia University, New York. Since 1974, she has been the Director and Chief Curator of The Renaissance Society at The University of Chicago, one of the oldest, most renowned and innovative contemporary art museums in the United States. As Curator of The Renaissance Society, Ghez has curated over 140 exhibitions and edited various publications in conjunction with these exhibitions. From 1999 to 2002 she served as co-curator of Documenta 11. Highly esteemed and prominent in her field, Ghez was awarded the 1996 Curators Grant from the Peter Norton Family Foundation, the 2002 International Lifetime Achievement Award for Curatorial Excellence from Bard College Center for Curatorial Studies, and honorary doctorates from The School of The Art Institute of Chicago in 2003 and The San Francisco Art Institute in 2006. Her record of advisory services is extensive, and includes Artpace, San Antonio (1997), the Carnegie International Advisory Committee (1998-99), the International Art Advisory Council for the Wexner Center for the Arts (1994-2006), the International Advisory Committee for the Office for Contemporary Art Norway (2003-2004) and the National Endowment for the Arts.

Susanne Ghez ging auf das Bryant College und studierte Kunstgeschichte an der University of California, Berkeley, sowie an der Columbia University, New York. Seit 1974 ist sie die Direktorin und leitende Kuratorin von The Renaissance Society at The University of Chicago, eines der ältesten, berühmtesten und innovativsten Museen für zeitgenössische Kunst in den USA. Als Kuratorin der Renaissance Society, hat Ghez über 140 Ausstellungen kuratiert und in Verbindung mit diesen Ausstellungen eine Reihe von Publikationen

herausgegeben. Von 1999 bis 2002 war sie Mit-Kurator der Documenta 11.
Hoch angesehen und herausragend auf ihrem Gebiet, erhielt Ghez 1996 den Curators Grant der Peter Norton Family Foundation, 2002 den International Lifetime Achievement Award for Curatorial Excellence des Bard College Center for Curatorial Studies, und Ehrendoktortitel des School of The Art Institute of Chicago im Jahr 2003 und des San Francisco Art Institute im Jahr 2006. Die lange Liste ihrer beratenden Tätigkeiten schließt Artpace, San Antonio (1997) ein, das Carnegie International Advisory Committee (1998-1999), den International Art Advisory Council for the Wexner Center for the Arts (1994-2006), das International Advisory Committee for the Office for Contemporary Art Norway (2003-2004) und die National Endowment for the Arts.

Photo Credit/Bildnachweis

Unless otherwise indicated images/Falls nicht anders angegeben Bilder
courtesy of the artist and David Zwirner, New York

"Alma Colectiva" Colecion Pepis y Aurelio Lopez Rocha p. 25
Charles Betlach, Private Collection p. 59
Collection/Sammlung Cleve Carney, Illinois p. 80
Collection Martin J. Friedman & Peggy L. Casey Friedman p. 62
Collection/Sammlung Rhona Hoffman, Chicago pp. 22, 29
Collection Toni and Danny Holtz p. 93
Collection Ilene Kurtz-Kretzschmar and Ingo Kretzschmar p. 90
Collection/Sammlung Aaron and/und Barbara Levine p. 77
Collection Damon McCarthy, California p. 20
Collection Lara and William McLanahan p. 89
Collection/Sammlung John and/und Amy Phelan p. 89
Collection/Sammlung Rodrigo Penafiel, Mexico City p. 69
Collection Arno and Danner Scheffler, Aspen p. 100
Collection Hanna Schouwink, New York pp. 58, 92
Collection Donna and Howard Stone pp. 14-17
Collection Penny Pritzker and Bryan Traubert, Chicago pp. 12-13, 27
Collection Toyota Municipal Museum of Art, Toyota City, Japan pp. 40, 52, 56, 60, 127
Collection/Sammlung Maurice van Valen, Amsterdam pp. 42, 50
Daros Collection/Sammlung Daros, Zürich p. 61
Hall Collection pp. 20, 64
Hauser & Wirth Collection, Switzerland pp. 14-17, 45-49
Jose Noe and Marcela Suro Collection, Guadalajara, Mexico p. 33
Private Collection, Amsterdam, The Netherlands p. 84
Private Collections, New York pp. 54, 64, 96
Private Collections/Privatsammlungen pp. 71, 88, 106-109

Photographers/FotografInnen

Roxanne Bank pp. 6, 102-103
Daniel Bayer pp. 104-105
Larissa Brantner James pp. 6, 114
Chuck Curry pp. 94-95
Niels Donckers p. 31
Brian Forrest p. 55
Steve Mundinger pp. 20-21, 25, 29, 86-89 (left/links), 93-95, 100, 117
Takeharu Ogai p. 30
Philippe Pirotte pp. 38-39
Peter Schalchi pp. 106-109
Mai Shimohana pp. 22, 82-83, 97-98
Yutaka Sone pp. 1-4, 68
Dominique Uldry pp. 62, 64, 69-71, 89 (right/rechts), 111-113
Tom Van Eynde pp. 12-17, 24, 26-27, 72-78, 80-81

**Acknowledgements/Danksagung
Studio Yutaka Sone**

The Renaissance Society at The University of Chicago
Susanne Ghez and/und Hamza Walker

Aspen Art Museum
Heidi Zuckerman Jacobson

Kunsthalle Bern
Philippe Pirotte

DAVID ZWIRNER, New York
David Zwirner and/und Hanna Schouwink

Rupert Burgess

Iwan Wirth

SPECIAL THANKS/BESONDERE DANKSAGUNG

The artist would like to extend his heartfelt thanks to
all those who have helped in the conception and realiza-
tion of the projects in this catalogue. Below, the artist
would like to especially thank and acknowledge the
following people and institutions for collaborating with
him in his respective projects.

Der Künstler möchte seinen tief empfunden Dank an
alle jene ausdrücken, die bei der Konzeption und
Realisierung der Projekte in diesem Katalog geholfen
haben. Weiterhin möchte der Künstler seinen beson-
deren Dank an die folgenden Personen und Institutionen
zum Ausdruck bringen, die mit ihm bei seinen jeweiligen
Projekten zusammengearbeitet haben.

Jiang Zhi Xian (Leicheng Stone Products Factory/
Leicheng Fabrik für Steinprodukte), Sky Burchard,
Michael Bauer, Larissa Brantner James and Lauren
Mollica, Min Nishihara, Lonnie Blanchard, Hitoshi
Nishiyama, Junko Shimada, Side2 Gallery, Jiang Sen
Hu, Tom Texas Holms, Benjamin Weissman, Peter
Doig, Hans Hohl, Ryan Miller, Don, David Amouyal,
Michael Eckrich, Jennifer Martin, Rob V, Steven Doe,
Rashad Butler, Oscar Santos, Laura Adams, Emerson
Jacobson, Jason Kraus, TJ

**Acknowledgements/Danksagung
The Renaissance Society at The University of Chicago**

At The Renaissance Society, *Forecast: Snow* was made
possible with funding from the Zell Family Foundation.
Additional exhibition sponsors include the Sara Lee
Foundation and the Japan Foundation.
The exhibition catalogue was generously funded by
Bert A. Lies, Jr. and Rosina Lee Yue, with additional
support from the W.L.S. Spencer Foundation.

Die Ausstellung in der Renaissance Society, *Forecast:
Snow*, wurde ermöglicht durch die finanzielle Unter-
stützung der Zell Family Foundation. Zusätzliche
Unterstützung erfuhr die Ausstellung von der Sara
Lee Foundation und the Japan Foundation.
Der Ausstellungskatalog wurde großzügig gefördert von
Bert A. Lies, Jr. und Rosina Lee Yue, sowie durch die
Unterstützung seitens der W.L.S. Spencer Foundation.

LENDERS/LEIHGEBER
James L. Cahn
Hall Collection/Sammlung Hall
Rhona Hoffman
Maurice van Valen
Rodrigo Penafiel
Martin J. Friedman and/und Peggy L. Casey Friedman
David Zwirner

THE RENAISSANCE SOCIETY
STAFF/MITARBEITERINNEN
Robert Bain, Lori Bartman, Jeremy Collatz, Susanne
Ghez, Petrova Giberson, Lise Haberman, Suzanne Kim,
Min Kyung Lee, Nora Liddell, Karen Reimer,
Mia Ruyter, Sara Slawnik, Hamza Walker, Steve Young

INSTALLATION TEAM/AUFBAUTEAM
John Almanza, Lindsay Bain, Ben Foch, Ben Gill,
Japeth Mennes, John Preus, Brandon Ross,
Brian Taylor, Philip Von Zweck

ASSISTANT/ASSISTENT STUDIO YUTAKA SONE
Michael Bauer

DAVID ZWIRNER, New York
David Zwirner, Hanna Schouwink, Gillian Ferguson,
Stephanie Daniel, Lori Salmon, Wendy White

**Acknowledgements/Danksagung
Aspen Art Museum**

X-Art Show was organized by the Aspen Art Museum
and was underwritten by Amy and John Phelan with
additional funding from the AAM National Council.
The catalogue was underwritten by Bert A. Lies,
Jr. and Rosina Lee Yue and Vicki and Kent Logan.
Additional support provided by Aspen Magazine.

X-Art Show wurde vom Aspen Art Museum organisiert
und finanziell gesichert von Amy und John Phelan
sowie der Unterstützung des AAM National Council.
Für den Katalog haben Bert A. Lies, Jr. und Rosina
Lee Yue sowie Vicki und Kent Logan Bürgschaften
übernommen. Zusätzliche Unterstützung erhielten wir
vom Aspen Magazine.

LENDERS/LEIHGEBER
Amy and/und John Phelan
David Zwirner, New York

ASPEN ART MUSEUM
STAFF/MITARBEITERINNEN
Heidi Zuckerman Jacobson, Roxanne Bank, Dasa
Bausova, Grace Brooks, Dara Coder, Josh Hirshberg,
Nicole Kinsler, Morley McBride, Kelly McGrath, Jared
Rippy, Christy Sauer, John-Paul Schaefer, Patrick
Storey, Pam Taylor, Matthew Thompson

SPECIAL THANKS/BESONDERE DANKSAGUNG
Laura Adams, David Amouyal, Michael Bauer,
Sky Burchard, Rashad Butler, Steven Deo, Michael
Eckrich, Hans Hohl, Heath Johnson, Jason Kraus,
Jennifer Martin, Damon McCarthy, Ryan Miller,
Oscar Santos, Patrick Storey

DAVID ZWIRNER, New York
David Zwirner, Hanna Schouwink, Gillian Ferguson,
Stephanie Daniel, Lori Salmon, Wendy White

**Acknowledgements/Danksagung
Kunsthalle Bern**

The Kunsthalle Bern wishes to thank the Japan Foundation and the Stanley Thomas Johnson Foundation for
making this exhibition and catalogue possible through
their support. We would also like to thank the City and
Canton of Bern, the SRG SSR Idée Suisse and the
Club 15 for their continuous commitment to the
Kunsthalle program.

Die Kunsthalle Bern ist es ein Bedürfnis, ihrer Dankbar-
keit gegenüber der Japan Foundation und der Stanley
Thomas Johnson Foundation Ausdruck zu verleihen für
ihre Unterstützung, die diese Ausstellung und den
Katalog ermöglicht hat. Ein weiterer Dank geht an die
Stadt und den Kanton Bern, sowie die SRG SSR Idée
Suisse und den Club 15 für ihr fortwährendes
Engagement für das Programm der Kunsthalle.

LENDERS/LEIHGEBER
Cleve Carney
Collection/Sammlung Hauser & Wirth, St. Gallen
Daros Collection/Sammlung Daros, Zürich
Martin J. Friedman and/und Peggy L. Casey Friedman
Hall Collection/Sammlung Hall
Rhona Hoffman
Aaron and/und Barbara Levine
Rodrigo Penafiel
John and/und Amy Phelan
Arno and/und Danner Schefler
Hanna Schouwink
Maurice van Valen
Private Collection/Privatsammlung

KUNSTHALLE BERN
STAFF/MITARBEITERINNEN
Pascale Keller, Susanne Kummer, Karin Minger,
Philippe Pirotte, Elfriede Schalit, Ines Schweinlin

INSTALLATION TEAM/AUFBAUTEAM
David Brühlmann, René Frick, Ivan König,
Werner Schmied, Aleardo Schüpbach, Working Tiger

ASSISTANTS/ASSISTENTINNEN STUDIO
YUTAKA SONE
Michael Bauer, Larissa Brantner James and/und
Lauren Mollica

SPECIAL THANKS/BESONDERE DANKSAGUNG
Studio Yutaka Sone, Chongwu, China
Studio Yutaka Sone, South Pasadena, CA
Reveal artprojects

DAVID ZWIRNER, New York
David Zwirner, Hanna Schouwink, Gillian Ferguson,
Stephanie Daniel, Lori Salmon, Wendy White

Colophon/Impressum

This catalogue has been published on the occasion of the exhibitions by Yutaka Sone *Forecast: Snow*, curated by Susanne Ghez, The Renaissance Society at The University of Chicago, 29.1 – 9.4.2006; *X-Art Show*, curated by Heidi Zuckerman Jacobson, Aspen Art Museum, 17.2. – 16.4.2006; *Like Looking for Snow Leopard*, curated by Philippe Pirotte, Kunsthalle Bern, 10.6 – 6.8.2006.

Diese Publikation erscheint anlässlich der Ausstellungen von Yutaka Sone *Forecast: Snow*, kuratiert von Susanne Ghez, The Renaissance Society at The University of Chicago, 29.1 – 9.4.2006; *X-Art Show*, kuratiert von Heidi Zuckerman Jacobson, Aspen Art Museum, 17.2. – 16.4.2006; *Like Looking for Snow Leopard*, kuratiert von Philippe Pirotte, Kunsthalle Bern, 10.6 – 6.8.2006.

Editors/HerausgeberInnen: Susanne Ghez, The Renaissance Society at The University of Chicago, Heidi Zuckerman Jacobson, Aspen Art Museum; Philippe Pirotte, Kunsthalle Bern
Coordinating Editor / Redaktion und Koordination: Nina Oeghoede
Authors/AutorInnen: Susanne Ghez, Philippe Pirotte, Hamza Walker, Benjamin Weissman, Heidi Zuckerman Jacobson
Photographers/FotografInnen: Roxanne Bank, Daniel Bayer, Chuck Curry, Niels Donckers, Brian Forrest, Steve Mundinger, Takeharu Ogai, Philippe Pirotte, Peter Schalchi, Mai Shimohana, Yutaka Sone, Dominique Uldry, Tom Van Eynde
Proofreading/Lektorat: Volker Ellerbeck, Karen Reimer, Nina Oeghoede, Elfriede Schalit
Translations/Übersetzungen: Volker Ellerbeck, Lynn George
Graphic Design / Gestaltung: Kim Beirnaert
Printed by / Gesamtherstellung: Die Keure NV, Brugge, Belgium/Belgien

© 2006 Yutaka Sone, The Renaissance Society at The Unversity of Chicago, Aspen Art Museum, Kunsthalle Bern, and the authors/und die AutorInnen.

Published by / Publiziert durch:

The Renaissance Society at The University of Chicago
5811 S. Ellis Avenue
Bergman Gallery, Cobb Hall 418
Chicago, Illinois 60637
Tel. +1 773 702 8670
Fax +1 773 702 9669
www.renaissancesociety.org

Aspen Art Museum
590 North Mill Street
Aspen, Colorado 81611
Tel. +1 970 925 8050
Fax +1 970 925 8054
www.aspenartmuseum.org

Kunsthalle Bern
Helvetiaplatz 1
3005 Bern, Schweiz
Tel. +41 31 3500040
Fax +41 31 3500041
www.kunsthalle-bern.ch

ISBN 3-85780-145-X
Printed in Belgium / Druck Belgien

We were in the Jungle—the Tiger and I, 2000
Acrylic on canvas / Acryl auf Leinwand
45.7 x 55.9 cm [18 x 22 in]